Optimal Location of Facilities

Gerard Rushton
Department of Geography
University of Iowa

This material was prepared with the support of National Science Foundation
Grants No. GJ-28456 and EPP71-01952. However, any opinions, findings,
conclusions, or recommendations expressed herein are those of the
author and do not necessarily reflect the views of NSF.

Copyright © 1979 Trustees of Dartmouth College

Published by  COMPress, Inc.
P.O. Box 102
Wentworth, N.H. 03282

ISBN 0-933694-10-5

All rights reserved except as noted below.

Except for the rights to material reserved by others, the Trustees of Dartmouth College and COMPress, Inc., hereby grant permission to all persons for use of this Work in the United States, its possessions, and Canada without charge after March 31, 1985, provided that written notice of such use is made to COMPress, Inc., and provided that any publication incorporating written materials covered by these copyrights contains the original copyright notice and a statement that the publication is not endorsed by the copyright owner or the National Science Foundation.

Manufactured in the United States of America

Table of Contents

Preface ix

Instructor's Introduction 1

Chapter 1 - The Location Problem

    1. Applications of Optimal Location Procedures 10
        A. The Private Sector 10
        B. Public Sector Location Problems 17
        C. Location Problems in Developing Countries . . . 26

    2. Classification of Location Problems 31
        A. The Problem 31
        B. Meaning of "Most Accessible" 32
        C. The Class of Location Problems 34
        D. Common Features of the Location Problem 35
        E. Interpretations of Supply Centers
           and Demand Points 36

    3. Methods for Solving Location Problems 37
        A. Exact Enumerative 37
        B. Exact Analytical 38
        C. Approximate Heuristic Algorithms 38
        D. Approximate Statistical Algorithms 39
        E. Exact Mathematical Programming 39
        F. Approximate Simulation Methods 40

Chapter 2 - The Single-Source Location Problem

    1. Location in Continuous Space 41
        A. The Problem 41
        B. Solution Methods 43
        C. Handworked Examples 54
        D. The Optimum Location in Chicago 58
        E. Homework Problems 59

Optimal Location of Facilities

    2. Locations on a Route Structure 64
        A. The Problem 64
        B. Solution Method 66
        C. Handworked Example 67
        D. Program ALLOC 70
        E. Transformation of the Distance Matrix 72
        F. Homework Problems 76

Chapter 3 - Multi-Facility Location in Continuous Space

        A. The Problem--Generalization of the
           One-Source Case 79
        B. Solution Methods 81
        C. Handworked Examples 87
        D. Programs for this Problem 96
        E. Homework Problems 100

Chapter 4 - Multi-Facility Location on a Network

    1. Minimizing Average Distance 107
        A. The Problem--Generalization of the One-Source
           Case for Minimizing Average Distance 109
        B. Solution Methods 110
        C. Handworked Examples 122
        D. Program ALLOC 128
        E. Tranformations of the Distance Matrix 133
        F. Homework Problems 134

    2. Minimizing the Maximum Distance to Closest
       Supply Centers in the System 135
        A. The Problem 135
        B. Solution Methods 137
        C. Handworked Example 138
        D. Program ALLOC 140
        E. Homework Problems 140

    3. Minimizing the Number of Centers Required for Every
       Demand Point to be Within a Critical Distance of a
       Supply Point 141
        A. The Problem 141
        B. Solution Methods 141
        C. Handworked Examples 142
        D. Homework Problems 145

    4. Minimizing Average Distance Subject to a
       Maximum Distance Constraint 145
        A. The Problem 145
        B. Solution Methods 147
        C. Handworked Example 147
        D. Program ALLOC 151
        E. Homework Problems 154

Contents

Chapter 5 - Shortest Paths through a Network

    A. The Problem 155
    B. Solution Methods 155
    C. Handworded Example 158
    D. Program SPA 159
    E. Homework Problems 163

References 165

Preface

In the period before computers became generally accessible to researchers and students, the principles of location were understood--and were taught--by the mechanism of constructing hypothetical environments with simple characteristics and postulating rules of behavior to rule therein. Mathematical and graphical analyses were then used to derive theorems about expected location patterns that would prevail. Important insights concerning industrial, agricultural and service location patterns were devised in this way (Isard,1956; Pred,1969; Webber, 1972). Introductory textbooks of human and economic geography, regional science and planning still introduce location theory by this method. But during the past decade a separate tradition of locational analysis has developed which, though it borrowed an occasional insight from conventional location theory, predominantly saw its task to be different. These analysts saw no reason to operate in hypothetical environments when the suggested analyses could, with the capability of modern computers, be performed on real environments. Furthermore, they saw no reason to postulate hypothetical behavior patterns with which to work when policy-makers whom they knew had alternative behaviors. They saw location theory, moreover, to be a prescriptive rather than a descriptive science, one that developed capabilities for finding location patterns that optimized a given set of criteria subject to constraints rather than one which looked backwards in an attempt to generalize about the characteristics of location patterns already in existence.

This book is written for the undergraduate student in the belief that this latter type of location theory represents the beginning of an academic literature that will surely grow and the foundation of methods for solving location problems that will be widely used in many practical situations in the years ahead. It seems important in the second sense that it represents the most positive use of the computer yet encountered to solve locational problems. Organizing geographical data banks and constructing and testing computational algorithms to find locational configurations that meet prescribed objectives is a pattern of activity that we will surely see more of in the future. An introduction to the literature and methods for finding optimal locations is thus an introduction to a pattern of thinking. It is this pattern of thinking and work that we wish to communicate here, and so throughout we stress the acquisition of skills for

Preface

performing these locational analyses. Even a casual glance at the chapters that follow will show that the solution of practical problems and the introduction to computer programs that accomplish the analyses described occupy a prominent place. I am trying to interest the student in solving problems. The most important homework problem at the end of each chapter is the unwritten one--the one the student identifies for himself and proceeds to collect data and to solve. I do this in the belief that the complexity of location problems is often missed and that it is in the solving of problems that most is learned. It has not been common to adopt this point of view in the study of location problems. The analysis of data in undergraduate classes is too often regarded as unnecessary, time-wasting and distracting from the essentials. There is surely the risk of missing the forest for the trees especially when a computer program sits like a black box waiting to transform data in form X into an analysis and problem solution. I have tried to minimize this risk by stressing small problems and hand calculations and I move to a discussion of the larger "packaged" programs only after the student has gained some experience with these smaller problems.

I have used these materials in three types of classes at the University of Iowa: Introductory Human Geography, Economic Geography and The Location of Service Activities. In the introductory class I place most importance on the intuitive solutions, on comparisons with the results of the computerized algorithms and on the handworked examples. The advanced class was introduced to these materials after several weeks of concern with traditional location theory literature. The contrast between this classical literature and the materials of this book in goals, methods and findings, is instructive. In the past two years I have found that a period of independent study toward the end of the semester affords an opportunity to the students to relate the two literatures and to perform an analysis on data that interests them. My classes have had students from a range of disciplines: Business, Hospital Administration, Urban Planning, General Liberal Arts, as well as Geography. The three weeks of independent study which must culminate in an analysis of a real problem and a written paper on it have provided them with a chance to relate the more abstract level of thinking in location theory to the problems and data with which they are familiar.

For efficiency and convenience, the computer programs can be put into a program library in load-module form. The student can then access any program by its acronym and gain immediate access to it in compiled form.

Instructors will note that this is not a comprehensive introduction to the facility location literature. It is too partial in the problems covered and the methods discussed to have any pretensions in that direction. It is a computer-oriented

Preface

supplement to a literature to fill a gap that has developed
because textbook expositions largely ignore the fact that the
practice of locational analysis has qualitatively as well as
quantitatively changed in the past decade as prescriptively
oriented analyses take their place beside more inductive
statistical analyses.

Hanover, New Hampshire
August 1973

Instructor's Introduction

This text is written for undergraduate students. It is derived from class notes developed for a senior-level course in the Department of Geography at The University of Iowa called <u>The Location of Services</u>. It uses several of the computer programs listed and documented in the monograph <u>Computer Programs for Location-Allocation Problems</u>. If the text is used as at The University of Iowa, students do not need to have access to this monograph but instructors will need to acquire copies of the FORTRAN source programs used in the text either from the listings contained in the monograph or from copies of the programs on tape which can be obtained either from the Geography Program Exchange in the Computer Institute for Social Science Research at Michigan State University, East Lansing, or from the Department of Geography at The University of Iowa.

---

1. Rushton, Gerard, M. F. Goodchild, and L. M. Ostresh, Jr. (eds.). <u>Computer Programs for Location-Allocation Problems</u>. Iowa City, Iowa: University of Iowa, Department of Geography, monograph no. 6, 1973, 321 pp.

Instructor's Introduction

This text is used in the second half of the semester course. The purpose of the course is to show that the location pattern of any activity influences the quality and quantity of services received and that methodologies exist to evaluate the locational effectiveness of any location pattern, to determine improvements that can be made and to compute location patterns that are optimum with respect to defined criteria. This text has been used to teach methodologies that are available to evaluate and to improve location patterns and to compute optimal patterns. In the course it follows an introductory section of approximately fifteen class meetings in which the processes that appear to be responsible for existing location patterns are discussed. In some cases these processes are presented in a narrative-descriptive framework (rather than analytical) in which forces that students have posited as being related to existing location patterns are discussed. Location patterns of physicians, hospitals and other health manpower are used as examples in this section. Also included in this first section of the course is a description of theoretical frameworks for explaining the location of service activities. These include central place theory, aspects of industrial-location theory and spatial diffusion theory. They are described as normative theories which optimize with respect to defined criteria operating in prescribed environmental conditions. This context allows for an easy and logical transition to the study in this text of alternative methods for finding optimal location patterns with the use of location-allocation algorithms. The class is taught that a symmetry exists between the objective functions which location-allocation algorithms are designed to optimize and location theories. That is, for every location theory there is an objective function--in principle if not in practice, and for every valid objective function a theoretical statement can be written. Unlike traditional location theories, however, which have generally been written for the conditions of uniform environments, location algorithms can be used to solve problems for a wide variety of environmental conditions.

This text is concerned with <u>types of location</u> problems and with <u>different methods</u> for their solution. It is oriented to students who want to acquire <u>specific skills</u> to solve location problems in the belief that many of them will have an opportunity in the future either to design a location pattern for some activity or to express an opinion on a proposed pattern. It is not difficult to convince students that knowledge of analytical methods for evaluating location patterns would be useful and, if known to them, would allow them to distinguish themselves from others who, in the absence of training in this area must settle for joining the crowd and attempt to assert a "solution" by pitting their opinion against that of others. With these skills they can argue in suitable cases for the separation of decisions <u>about criteria</u> to be used in finding optimal location patterns from the <u>methodology</u> to be used to find the location pattern that

Instructor's Introduction   4

optimizes with respect to that criteria. In cases of public
activities or activites with respect to which the public have a
compelling interest, it is a public rather than a professional
decision as to which criteria should be used; but it is a
professional decision to choose the appropriate method to
implement the criteria. After learning about solution methods,
students are soon able to understand that computer methods are
usually the most practical way to implement these methods.

   The text is designed to introduce solution methods through
small hand worked examples before it expects students to compute
solutions for larger problems with computer aid. In the course
"The Location of Services," students are asked to complete these
examples of the algorithms before proceeding to use the packaged
computer programs on larger data sets. These data sets are
prepared by the instructor and placed on a computer disc to
facilitate student use and to reduce costs. For the same reasons
the programs themselves are compiled and put in load-module form
on the same disc. In each case students are given a small pack
of approximately six pre-punched computer cards containing the
job control and accounting information for the problem and in the
first application they are asked to prepare control cards to
place behind this pack so that particular problems will be
solved. After these skills have been established, students are
asked to prepare part or all of the data required for other
problems. They are asked to prepare a term paper describing a

locational problem, the area in which they have studied this problem and the results of their analysis.

Other courses may want to give greater or less emphasis to solution methods. If less emphasis is planned, an instructor might decide to pass quickly over many of the hand-worked examples and instead be satisfied with having accomplished formal classroom explanation of the methods. The text is designed so that instructors can move more rapidly to the use of the packaged programs. Instructors of courses which have a marked orientation to computational methods and to the applications of computers in geography may want their students to use the monograph from which the packaged programs are drawn as an additional text on the grounds that it does include a more formal description of the algorithms, their listing, and sample input data as well as a number of additional location-allocation algorithms that are not discussed in this text.

Chapter 1 - The Location Problem

In the quest for knowledge in social science, it is usual to characterize a universe of objects that one wants to know more about, to gather a random sample representative of that universe and so to generalize about it. So common is this approach that it can be called a paradigm of the scientific method. A method, after all, is a procedure that works so well that one wants to use it again. The drawback of a good method, however, is that one is tempted to ask only those kinds of questions that the method can answer. And so it was with the problem of location. For in gathering those random samples and then in investigating their inter-correlations, location is the one variable almost invariably ignored. Later, questions did begin to be raised about the degree to which the variability in a data sample is attributable to the location of the points. Further, what if their locations were changed? Would the values of the variables remain the same?

Though such questions begin to take location into account, they still view it in the passive role of observation. Then researchers began to ask a more positive class of questions. If one wanted a certain variable or variables to attain a maximum or a minimum value, could certain objects be relocated to achieve this? If so, where should these locations be?

We have now categorized three types of questions. First, the question of making valid statements about the contents of areas; secondly, the question of the influence of location and locational relationships on the values of data measured at different points; finally, the question of optimally locating a set of objects so that some variable or variables will achieve a maximum or a minimum value. It is with the last question that this book is concerned.

In adopting the question of the best location pattern to meet specified requirements, we leave descriptive science and adopt the stance of prescriptive science. The prime concern is no longer to explain things as they are but to make rational assertions about how they should be. Here the concern is with the locations of things. It is a concern for the variety of considerations that can be optimized and the kinds of methods available to find the optimal locations.

This approach to location problems is timely, for the pressures of expanding populations in relation to finite land resources are demanding new approaches to locational decisions, not only those related to the location of farms, factories and service institutions, but also those regarding the distribution of new urban centers, the spatial structure of present and future urban areas, and the spatial interactions of their inhabitants. Traditional geographic theory emphasized the laissez-faire approach to location decisions where commercial and other private interests were primary, and where implications for the public of the location choices of individual firms were rarely considered. More recently the terms of reference of locational decision-making have changed in rather significant ways. They have been broadened in scope to include welfare considerations in the private sector and have become concerned with the location of public facilities. This shift has opened many new avenues of research, leading to the development of new insights and theories. In studying the subject of optimum locations, it is better to organize our thoughts around the types of problems that exist rather than the areas of application of these methods. Thus, later in this chapter we will develop a classification of location problems and indicate where in the text each problem is discussed. Before developing this classification, let us consider the range of practical problems which require the methods described in this text for their solution.

1. Applications of Optimal Location Procedures

A. The Private Sector

In the private sector of the economy, locations are chosen that are in harmony with the overall objectives of the owners. It is customary to ascribe profit maximization as the usual primary objective and in this context location enters as a cost in two senses. First, in controlling the level of transportation costs incurred--both for assembling materials and distributing the product to consumers, and second, in controlling the level of operating costs for the level of production required at that location. Consider yourself the owner of a firm producing a good required in different amounts at different locations. Let us pose a series of graduated questions; that is, questions posed in an order that generally becomes more realistic but also more difficult to solve. In all cases locations are variable but the nuances of the different problems posed are intended to demonstrate the subtleties that surround the problem of precise problem definition. All problems are, however, related to that of accomplishing a saving in a firm's distribution costs. A Canadian study estimated that the cost of storing and transporting goods amounts to approximately six percent of their gross national product, representing 15 per cent of the total expenses of the average firm, (Drysdale and Sandiford, 1969). Improving the locational efficiency of the

The Location Problem

spatial organization of the firm hence holds promise for making a substantial saving.

Case 1. You are beginning production of a product in which production costs are the same from one location to another. You have estimated the potential demand for your product at different locations, have decided that one factory is required for production of this good and so wish to find the location for it that will minimize your cost of getting your product to the consumers. With the methods described in Chapter 2, Section 1, you are able to compute an iso-cost map showing the location of the optimum place and the degree to which costs will vary from the optimum point for all other possible locations of your factory. An example of such a map is shown in Fig. 1.1 where the cost map refers to the cost of supplying a unit of your production to everyone in the continental United States (as they were distributed in 1948). Harris found that the national market of the United States could be served by least (land) transport cost from Fort Wayne, Indiana. The iso-cost lines indicate the percent increase for serving the market from all other locations over the cost from Fort Wayne. These can be regarded as the penalties associated with not being in the best location.

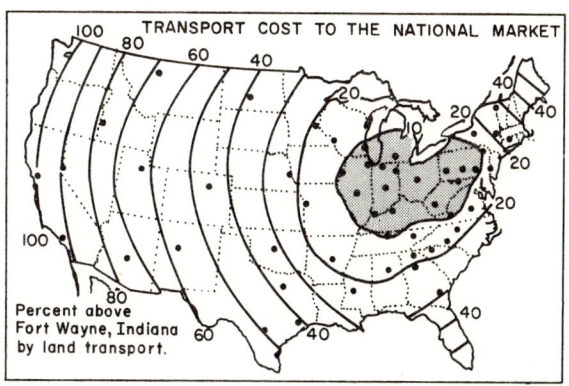

Fig. 1.1. Transport cost of serving the entire U.S. market in 1950 from a single point.

Source: Harris, 1954, p. 324.

Reproduced by permission from the Annals of the Association of American Geographers, Volume 44, 1954.

The second example refers to the cost of distributing a unit product to every farm household in the United States owning a tractor. This is a conceivable way in which a manufacturer of tractors might estimate the location pattern of potential demand for his product. He would have no illusions, of course, that he would actually be supplying every farm household with a new tractor but, on the other hand, he may have no reason to believe that the proportion of farm households in any area who might want to purchase his product would vary from one area to another. This being the case, he would find his best location with respect to the location pattern of all farm households. Harris, who computed the solution (Fig. 1.2) remarks how, either by accident or design, the actual location of one of the largest

The Location Problem

tractor manufacturers is located at the optimum location he had computed.

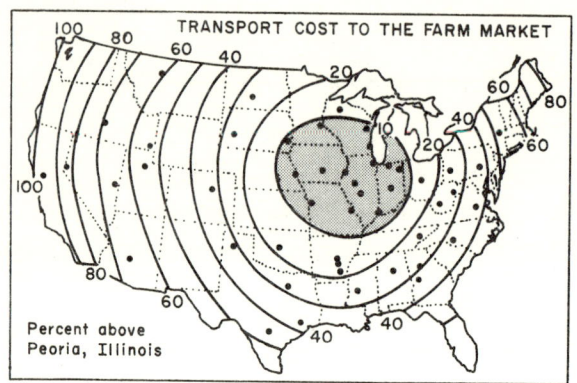

Fig. 1.2. Transport costs of serving the U.S. market for tractors from a single point.

Source: Harris, 1954, p. 342.

Reproduced by permission from the Annals of the Association of American Geographers, Volume 44, 1954.

Case 2. Your present plant is operating at capacity and you want to locate a second plant so that the total transport charges to the market from both plants is a minimum. Assumptions are that production costs do not vary between locations and that a new plant should be located rather than having the capacity of the existing plant expanded.

Case 3. You are considering locating two new warehouses in a certain territory. Where should they be located so that their transportation costs of marketing their produce is minimized? Here it is assumed before the analysis begins that the relative cost of operating the warehouse does not vary between locations.

It is a more difficult locational problem because there is now not one cost surface on which to compute and find the minimum value but as many cost surfaces as there are unique combinations of two locations in the area to be examined.

Case 4.

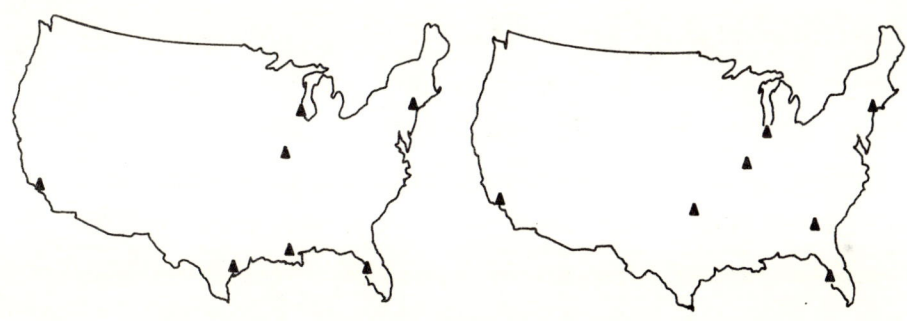

Fig. 1.3.

Actual location of plants
of Anheuser-Busch Brewing Co.

Optimal locations of plants of
Anheuser-Busch Brewing Co.

Source: Leamer, 1968.

This problem is exemplified in the location pattern of the plants of the Anheuser-Busch Brewing Company (Fig. 1.3). Here the locations of the plants that would minimize the distribution costs of reaching the consumers in the areas closest to each plant were determined using one of the computational methods described in Chapter 3. In this problem all seven locations were regarded as variable so that the number of different ways these seven could have been located is clearly enormous, yet the computational process described in Chapter 3 to solve this problem requires only a few seconds on a modern computer to reach an estimate of the location pattern required.

Case 5. Find the number of warehouses, their locations and the places they should supply such that total costs of maintenance, operation, and shipments are a minimum. The per unit operation costs, moreover, vary from one location to another. This location problem was studied for the RCA Victor company in Canada (a medium-sized company manufacturing home appliances). In Fig. 1.4 two solutions are compared. They differ in that they show the location pattern for two different fixed costs of maintaining warehouses in the system. As this fixed cost increases, and it becomes more economical to incur increased transportation charges in order to save some of the fixed cost charges, the solution location pattern becomes more centralized. A comparison with the actual locations of the company's warehouses for the appropriate level of fixed costs showed that the company was operating too many warehouses and that it could save 7% of the costs it was incurring in the distribution process by adopting the computed solution (Fig. 1.5).

W Indicates the seven warehouse locations. The fixed cost equals $6000.

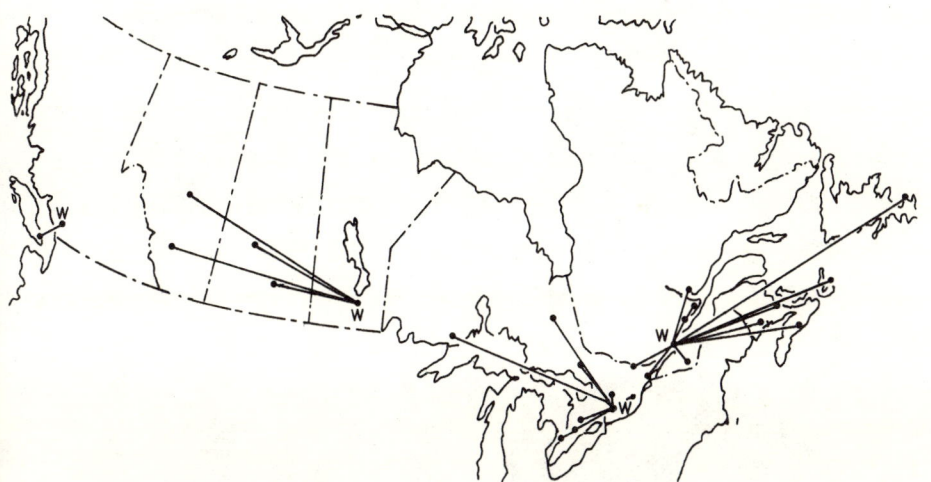

W Indicates the four warehouse locations. The fixed cost equals $16,000.

Fig. 1.4. Optimum number and location of warehouses for the RCA-Victor Company for two levels of fixed cost.

Source: Drysdale and Sandiford, 1969.

The Location Problem

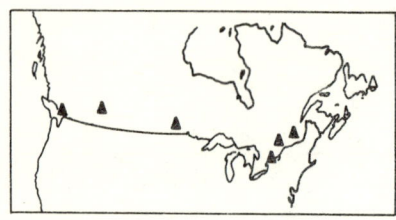 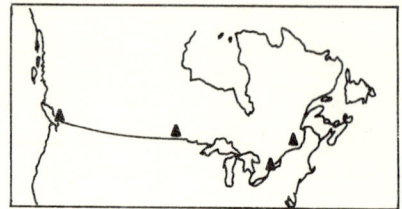

a) Actual seven locations
Total Costs per year:
426,568

b) Optimum four locations
Total Costs per year:
399,145

Fig. 1.5. Comparison of optimum with actual locations of warehouses of the RCA-Company.

The examples in this section illustrate the sensitivity of the profit maximizing goals of firms to different location patterns of their facilities. The result of this sensitivity is at least a periodic, if not a continuous, evaluation of the efficiency of their location pattern. If transport costs change or the pattern of demand or locations of materials used in the production process changes, these will be reflected in the cost/revenue position of the firm. Questions would normally be raised at this point and decisions about new locations or relocations would be made. For a case study of such a process for a major manufacturing firm, see Whitman and Schmidt, 1966.

B. <u>Public-Sector Location Problems</u>

Location decisions in the public sector are more difficult to optimize because of the variety of considerations often deemed to be relevant in determining the best location. In the public sector, also, inter-group conflicts often develop over location decisions so that the decision finally made represents a compromise between the wishes of the groups; favoring, perhaps, one or the other group in proportion to the political influence each wields. Many public-sector locations must be made within the highly competitive bidding process for sites that prevails within the city so that the question of the best location also involves a ranking process with regard to the relative priorities of the different sectors. Many public sector location patterns have come into being over the years in response to these complex forces. In view of the forces that would rise up if any attempts were made to thoroughly revise the pattern, questions of optimal location for the system as a whole are academic questions. The more meaningful question is thus to find the incremental changes that should be made to the system--either additions to or deletions from the system. Sometimes these are made within the perspective of a long-range plan for the future with an important short-run question being the optimal sequencing of the incremental changes to the system. An example of the difficulties of implementing even small changes to a public location pattern occurred in New York in January 1973 (The New Yorker, Jan 6, 1973, p. 64). A research study by The New York RAND Institute had recommended the closing down of some fire stations and the reallocation to other stations in the city of the firemen stationed there. New York's fire stations had changed little over the past fifty years even though some areas

The Location Problem

had gained and others lost population. The statistics on calls indicated that some stations were grossly overworked and others were underutilized and so the RAND study had recommended some modest changes in the location pattern. Their proposal (which Mayor Lindsay adopted) was designed to least disrupt the present system, yet do most to remedy its deficiencies. Nevertheless, the firemen of the city of New York responded by organizing a protest rally in Central Park and other citizen groups picketed the areas surrounding the stations to be closed in an attempt to put pressure on City Hall to change its mind. City Hall, in this case, held to its original decision and has since pressed ahead with the deployment and implementation of a computerized dispatching system which automatically evaluates the status of all fires in the city and the location pattern of the reserve units. If the analysis shows that some areas are not adequately protected in the event of the outbreak of new fires, the computer searches for the closest available equipment that can be temporarily relocated without loss of protection to the area where it is currently located, and recommends its relocation. This analysis is repeated every five minutes, twenty-four hours a day, by a computer, which, in the intervals between the analyses, is assigned to work on other jobs!

Ordinary and Emergency Public Services. It is useful to draw a distinction between emergency services where minimum standards are usually set and are guaranteed to everyone and ordinary services where a measure of "overall performance" is often the guiding standard. The criteria used to evaluate locational decisions for the two types of service are usually different. Emergency services include certain kinds of medical attention including ambulance dispatching, police and fire protection, vehicle breakdown services and some forms of welfare services. Ordinary services include facilities associated with health, education and welfare. Even though all agree that the public's access to such essential services is important, it is nevertheless usual for other considerations to become paramount in the locational decision process. The conflict often arises out of the fact that the best location from the point of view of the producer of the service is different from the best location from the consumer's viewpoint. This same conflict occurs in the private sector, of course; but there a commensurate unit in the form of costs and revenues exists which can be used to adjudicate or compromise between the different locations. In the public sector, however, such a commensurate unit does not exist. Indeed, for the consumer access side of locational evaluation, no unit exists that is generally agreed upon (see discussion in next section). In such situations where a hard and fast measure is available on the one hand (the production side) and a rather nebulous "measure" of consumer access on the other, it should not surprise us to learn that the production consideration is the one that is most often served. For an example, study the four maps of Iowa, the first showing the locations of Iowa hospitals in

The Location Problem

1971 (Hindes, 1971). Since 1965 when the first intensive coronary care facility was installed in an Iowa hospital, each year has seen additional hospitals receive funds for setting up such units. The federal program which provided some of the funds for this purpose specifically stated that the units should be located so that the population would have access to them and, more specifically, that the goal should be to have them located so that everyone would be within thirty minutes driving time of a unit.

22   Optimal Location of Facilities

Fig. 1.6. Iowa hospitals in 1971.

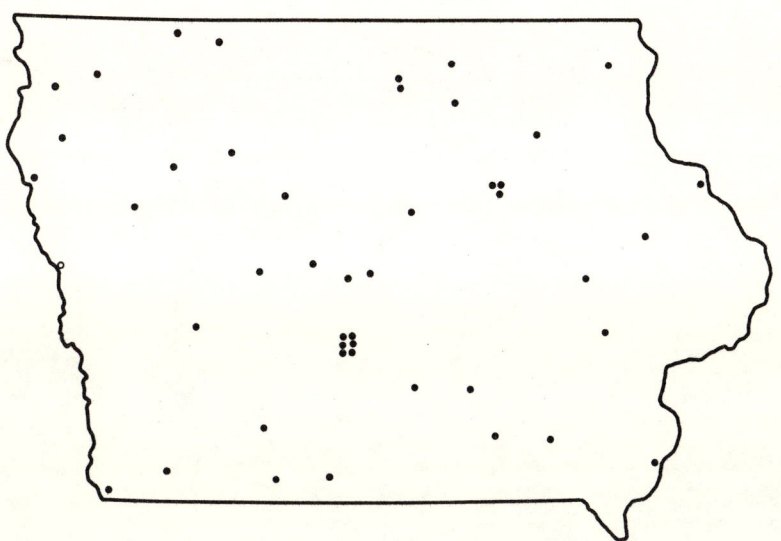

Fig. 1.7. Iowa hospitals with coronary care units, 1971.

The Location Problem   23

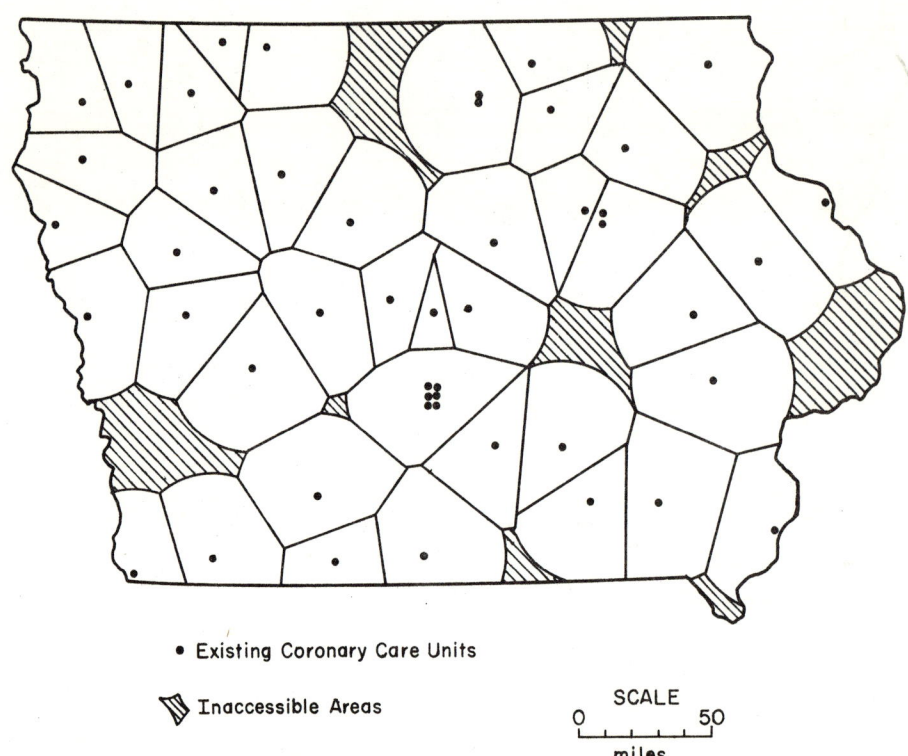

Fig. 1.8. Actual service areas of Iowa CCU's-1971

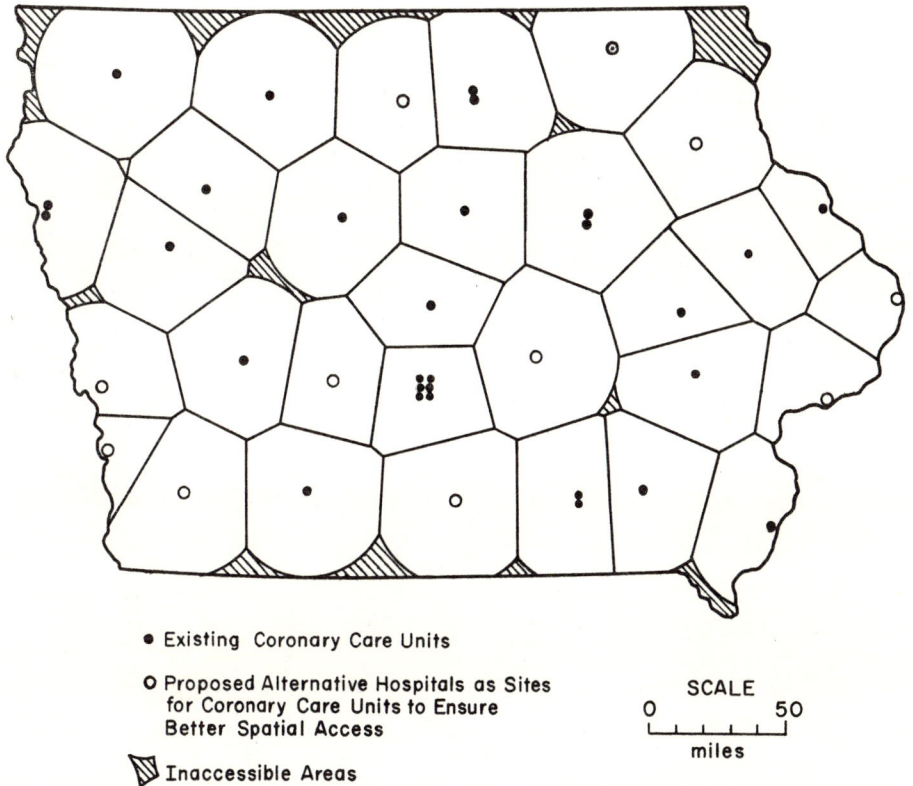

Fig. 1.9. Suggested normative distribution of Iowa CCU's.

Figure 1.7 shows that by 1971 the actual pattern of ICCU's that had evolved was clustered, and Figure 1.8 shows further that the criterion of having everyone within thirty minutes driving time had not been realized in 1971 even though many times the minimum number of units theoretically needed to meet the criteria had been exceeded. The fourth figure (Fig. 1.9) illustrates this point by showing that, with a minimum of relocations, a far more efficient location pattern could have been organized. The procedure by which these units had come to Iowa had emphasized the initiatives of the production units in the form of providing matching funds and applying for the federal funds. The intended efficiency of the set of ICCU's as a system written into the authorization program for the funds turned out in this case to be merely a platitude and the evidence suggests that consumer access considerations must have been ignored--yet another instance of the neglect of the location variable alluded to earlier.

Considering the complexity of the location decision process for public facilities the role of optimizing approaches to evaluating locations will often be to set standards against which to measure the departures in the locational patterns that emerge from the political process of decision-making. Through experience more decision makers are coming to the realization that methods for finding optimal locations represent a powerful aid in the process. Some still fear that a legitimate part of their authority is being taken from them when a computer is assigned the task of developing a location plan for facilities under their jurisdiction. Others with more experience and insights into the proper role of men and machines realize that the machine is but a taskmaster evaluating data according to a process programmed for it. With this realization, unacceptable "solutions" are evaluated not to be changed to some other location pattern in an ad hoc way, but with the purpose of deciding exactly what criteria should have been optimized so that the computer can be reprogrammed to find a more satisfactory solution. Thus, the area of responsibility of the decision-maker shifts in a qualitatively significant direction. Instead of spending time finding solutions to meet their specifications, decision-makers would spend their time more productively if they were to define more carefully the criteria that the location pattern should meet and leave to the computer and the more professional location analyst the job of finding the best location pattern that meets their specifications.

C. Location Problems in Developing Countries

In developing countries the same range of location problems exists as in developed countries, but certain differences cause us to consider location problems in such countries in a class of their own. Five considerations are relevant.

(1) Undeveloped transport systems. A consequence of poor transport systems is that to provide any level of functional

service to a population, facilities have to be located closer together than in situations where better transportation conditions prevail. This easily recognized fact forces policy-makers to examine the "trade-offs" between investments in new facilities to provide an acceptable level of service and investments in improved transport systems that will lead to the same acceptable level of service to be achieved with a smaller investment in facilities. In developed countries the state of the transport system is more frequently taken as a given and the facility location problem is considered to be an independent problem. In developing countries, on the other hand, developing the transport system and solving the facility location problem are frequently interdependent problems. A common situation is one in which transport planners know where to improve the transport system--providing they are told where the many new facilities will be located; and the locators of facilities know where to locate their facilities providing they are told where the new transport links and other improvements will be! Unfortunately, good methods for simultaneously evaluating the facility location pattern and the transport system to determine the best location and timing for both types of investments do not yet exist.

(2) <u>Integration of multi-facility location patterns</u>. In many parts of developing countries a wide range of public

services is introduced to backward regions at one time. So instead of taking the presently existing location of facilities and fitting an additional facility pattern to it, the problem is one of developing an optimum pattern for a system of facilities.

(3) Serving demand or creating demand? Many studies in developed countries take the existing pattern of utilization of a public service as the measure of the spatial distribution of needs, but when a service is being introduced to an area where nothing comparable has previously existed, such measures of need are clearly unsuitable. Facility location patterns in such circumstances perform the role of creating their demand and so it is sometimes argued that their location pattern should be organized to generate the most use.

An example where a pre-existing location pattern is modified and a new system introduced is shown in Fig. 1.10. Fifty market centers are identified which received loans from the World Bank in 1972 to upgrade their marketing facilities. The loan of approximately $12,000,000 was to provide modern facilities for agricultural marketing, including fair weighing of produce, all weather storage facilities, amenities for the farmers using the market, and improved transport facilities to surrounding areas. The fifty markets receiving the loans were chosen from about 300 pre-

The Location Problem

Fig. 1.10. Bihar markets map

existing markets, and although the government report (Government of Bihar Report, 1972, p. 37) is not clear on exactly how these locations were selected, it is clear that the current level of activity was an important criterion. In view of the clustered nature of the proposed pattern one is forced to question whether some alternative location pattern might not have benefited more farmers in the area and even made a higher monetary return on the investment.

(4) Remedying the mis-allocations of former colonial systems. One of the problems with solving conventionally defined location problems in a developing country is that the past pattern of development constrains the solution proposed to such a degree that the solution reinforces the general features of the pre-existing pattern of activities. But this pattern often reflects the goals and needs of former colonial powers whose criteria for the pattern of activities they presided over differed radically from that held by the country after independence.

(5) Equalization of levels of welfare. Many developing countries are concerned about equalizing the different levels of welfare prevailing throughout their area. Facility location planning is often seen as one of the means of reaching this goal.

In summary, there appears to be the need in most developing countries to broaden the scope of facility location planning to integrate such plans with other plans (particularly in transportation) and to use facility planning to achieve national goals that usually have no counterpart in the developed world. We now turn to the range of criteria that can be proposed in any location problem.

2. Classification of Location Problems

A. The Problem

People are distributed unevenly in earth space and they must obtain many kinds of goods and services from facilities located at widely separated places. They have an obvious interest in the locations of these facilities being "most accessible" to them. For goods and services whose provision is at public expense, the people responsible for locating the facilities have an interest in providing the best service within budget restrictions. That is, other things being the same, they too have an interest in locating the facilities to be "most accessible." Given this apparent identity of interest, we thus face the challenge of specifying what conditions a location pattern must have to be "most accessible." We then face the further problem of showing how location patterns meeting these conditions should be found.

B. Meaning of "Most Accessible"

A number of alternative definitions of "most accessible" have been proposed and the methods devised to meet the requirements of each definition invariably differ. These definitions will be expanded in the separate instructional units which follow, but they are briefly: <u>Definition - A location pattern is most accessible to people when, for any given number of facilities</u>:

(1) The total of the distances of all people from their closest facility is minimum. Call this the "aggregate distance minimization" criterion. This is also equivalent to "minimizing `average distance'." Call this the `average distance' criterion;

(2) The farthest distance of people from their closest facility is minimum. Call this the "minimax distance" criterion;

(3) The number of people in the proximal area surrounding each facility is approximately equal. Call this the "equal assignment" criterion;

(4) The number of people in the proximal area surrounding each facility is always greater than a specified number. Call this the "threshold constraint" criterion;

(5) The number of people in the proximal area surrounding each facility is never greater than a specified number. Call this the "capacity constraint" criterion.

Which definition one should use in any application will vary according to the preferences of the decision-maker. Even the same decision-maker might choose different definitions for different applications. To further complicate matters, some decision-makers may decide to mix several definitions to make an essentially new criterion. For example, to cite one popular hybrid definition:

> (6) A location pattern is most accessible to people when, for any given number of facilities, the total of the distances of all people from their closest facility is minimized subject to the constraint that no person is more than a specified distance from their closest facility.

This definition combines definitions (1) and (2) above. Similarly, other combinations are possible and appropriate in given circumstances.

Sometimes the problem is "inverted," that is, it is restated in such a way that some aspect of the problem which was explicit in the definitions above becomes the variable to be solved for. For example, the problem might be defined as:

> (7) Find the minimum number and their respective locations of a set of facilities such that the farthest distance of anyone from his closest facility is less than a specified distance.

These definitions do not exhaust the possibilities; they merely illustrate the variety of conditions which impinge on the meaning of "accessibility," especially when this concept is applied to aggregates of people. The definitions above can be grouped into classes according to whether they are oriented toward equalizing individual accessibilities, (2) and (7); toward imposing a constraint on the internal facility characteristics

(3), (4) and (5); or toward reaching an aggregate or "net" benefit condition.

Questions:

1. Choose an application for which each definition would be the most "appropriate" definition of "most accessible."

2. Which definitions would be most appropriate for finding the optimum location patterns for: a) fire stations in a city; b) U.S. Post Offices; c) regional shopping center; d) neighborhood shops; e) police stations; f) little "city halls"; g) a warehouse distribution system.

C. The Class of Location Problems

Because of these many interpretations of the location problem, not one but many problems exist and each interpretation alters the mathematical character of the problem. Thus location problems are solved by a variety of approaches, each designed to meet the specifications of the particular interpretation of the problem.

Problems differ also in the size of the data set which is relevant to particular applications. This difference also leads to different mathematical approaches to the same problem since approaches that are feasible for small data problems, commonly become infeasible for larger data bases.

The nature of the data set available also conditions the approach to the solution that is adopted. Data may be available for administrative areas of identical or widely different sizes and the areas may be identified by locational coordinates which may be Cartesian coordinates, latitude and longitude coordinates; or some other coordinate system. Areas may be identified by names and distances, or costs between all pairs of areas may be known. Alternatively, distances may be known only for links between directly connected places and distances between all pairs of points would have to be computed before many of the approaches to optimal location could be adopted. In some cases data may be available as a trend-surface function in which density of the data in question is expressed as a function of location coordinates.

D. *Common Features of the Location Problems*

Despite these differences of problem interpretation, data size and kind, all approaches combine two distinct principles. In all cases location is variable--that is, location must be found and in all cases some procedure must be used for allocating the points to be served to particular sources. These two principles are used to characterize facility location problems as LOCATION-ALLOCATION PROBLEMS.

In some cases the allocations are the result of free choice between the demand points and the potential suppliers. At other times, the demand points are assigned to facilities. Solutions to the location problem must work within the allocating principle that is relevant for the matter being studied. Some solution methods can be readily adapted to a variety of allocation patterns, others are less versatile.

E. <u>Interpretations</u> <u>of</u> <u>Supply</u> <u>Centers</u> <u>and</u> <u>Demand</u> <u>Points</u>

Throughout this book we refer to the places to be located as "supply centers" and the places with fixed locations as "demand points." This manner of naming has the advantage of giving a substantive meaning to the problem at every stage but it carries with it the danger that interpretations of the problem where these terms are not relevant may be missed. Consider this problem, for example, locate p milk collection points for dairy farmers selling their milk to a dairy so that the average time consumed by the farmers in taking their milk to the closest collection center is a minimum. In this problem it is the collection centers that have variable locations and the farmers who have fixed locations. This is a location-allocation problem because there are variable locations and allocations from the fixed locations to them, and it is these interactions which must, in fact, be minimized. Although in this problem the collection centers are demand points and the farms are supply centers, in our nomenclature the collection centers are supply points and the farms are demand points. Note that always the fixed locations are called demand points and the variable locations are called supply points irrespective of which is physically supplying which. The variable being minimized is the interaction between the two sets and for that purpose the direction of interaction is irrelevant. Many other examples could be given. Manufacturing plants that are being located with respect to raw material sources that have fixed locations would be regarded as "supply points" receiving the raw materials from the "demand points" though it is clear that the actual interactions are the reverse of this.

3. Methods for Solving Location Problems

A. Exact Enumerative

For small location problems an exact solution can be obtained by computing all possible solutions and selecting the best. In one of the simplest problems where the demand points are to be served by two supply centers, it is clear that the best solution--whatever it is--will show one group of the demand points going to one supply center and the remainder going to the other. If one found all the ways the demand points could combine into two separate groups and then found the optimal location for each group, the best solution found would be the solution sought. The drawback to this approach is the extremely large number of combinations of the demand points that are possible. With as few as fifty demand points and five supply points, the number of different combinations of the demand points is in the billions.

B. Exact Analytical

These methods cover the cases where, by the use of a computation or by a series of computations, one can know that the solution sought has been found. In the first section of Chapter 2, for example, we show an iterative series of computations for which a proof exists that the location with the desired properties will always be found.

C. Approximate Heuristic Algorithms

These methods comprise sequences of computations which it is believed will frequently lead to the desired solution. This belief is founded on the logic of the computations and is frequently supported by extensive empirical experience. Unlike the exact analytical methods, no proof exists that heuristic methods will find the best possible solution. The popularity of these methods results from their usefulness in situations where exact analytical methods for the problem studied either do not exist, or are prohibitively expensive, or when a range of possible "solutions" is desired from which policy-makers may make a selection using criteria that had not been (and perhaps could not be) formalized in the algorithm used.

D. Approximate Statistical Algorithms

These methods are statistical in that they draw samples from a universe of solutions and use statistical estimation theory to estimate the confidence that the best solution found is among the best solution possible. These methods have fallen in popularity in recent years as other methods have proven able to find solutions that are as good or better using less computer time. People were tempted to use these methods because they were easy to program for computer solution. This was especially so before the source codes of alternative computerized algorithms had been published and extensively described.

E. Exact Mathematical Programming

Approaches here consist of demonstrating that the particular location problem studied belongs to a class of problems for which a structured approach to finding an exact solution exists. The attempt is thus to capitalize on previously developed and tested computational approaches by showing that the structure of the location problem is isomorphous with some better-known problem. It has been shown that several kinds of location problems can be arranged as linear programming problems so that after the data have been formulated in a suitable form and the constraints written, the linear programming technique will usually yield a solution. Further progress in this area can be expected as the techniques of mathematical programming are refined and become better known.

F. **Approximate Simulation Methods**

Especially when the demand distribution is probabilistically defined, so that timing characteristics of the system being developed are important, simulation models are constructed that imitate the major features of the system modeled. One study, for example, (Savas, 1969), assessed the desirability of reallocating the number of ambulances dispatched from two locations by simulating the occurrences of calls in the area to be serviced and allocating the ambulances to serve them. Implications for the level of servicing attained under various combinations at the two locations were calculated and the results used to recommend the optimal combination of the ambulances between the two locations.

In this book, no attempt has been made to systematically cover every computational method that has been used for the location problem. In fact, discussion of methods in a comparative sense has been given only passing attention since the main theme of the book is recognizing the types of location problems that exist and applying a few computational principles to them. We hope to show that an understanding of these few principles is sufficient to attain working ability to solve a large variety of location problems. Issues of choice across the great diversity of solution methods can be resolved only after the full substantive literature of location-allocation has been reviewed.

Chapter 2 - The Single-Source Location Problem

We make the distinction in this chapter between the case where the location to be determined may be found anywhere within the area--literally an infinity of points; and the case where locations must be chosen from points lying on a route-structure of roads and connecting paths.

1. Locations in Continuous Space

A. The Problem

For problems in continuous space, optimum locations cannot be found by direct comparison of a set of all possible locations. Rather, a computational strategy must be developed that will swiftly and unambiguously lead to the desired location.

Let the objective function to be optimized be the average distance of the points to be served from the unknown source location. Mathematically, this may be written as:

$$\text{minimize } z = \sum_{i=1}^{n} w_i d(p_i, X) \tag{1}$$

This should be read as: find the values for X (the unknown location coordinates) such that the sum of the weighted distances from all demand points to the location X is minimum. Each ith point has associated with it a number of units that must be served (w_i), referred to here as weight.

The simplest case is where all demand locations lie along a line. For this case X, the unknown location, has one coordinate only (since the problem lies in one dimension), and distances may be defined as:

$$d(p_i, X) = |p_i - X| \quad (i = 1, 2 \ldots, n) \tag{2}$$

and the objective function may be written as:

$$\text{minimize } z = \sum_{i=1}^{n} |p_i - X| \tag{3}$$

Where the demand locations are scattered in a plane of two dimensions, the distances may be defined in one of two ways.

(i) The city-block metric

If it is assumed that movement between two points may only occur in two directions, then if the Cartesian coordinates axes are the same as these directions, distances may be defined as:

$$d(p_i, X) = |p_{i1} - x_1| + |p_{i2} - x_2| \tag{4}$$

This is equivalent to movement along city streets in a city with a rectangular street net or distances between towns in much of the mid-west where roads typically follow the property dividing

The Single-Source Location Problem

lines which owe their origin to the rectangular land-survey system of townships and ranges. For such a distance metric the objective function may be written:

$$\text{minimize } z = \sum_{i=1}^{n} w_i |p_{i1} - x_1| + \sum_{i=1}^{n} w_i |p_{i2} - x_2| \tag{5}$$

This metric is often called the city-block or manhattan metric.

(ii) The air-line metric

If it is assumed that movement between two points may take place directly (air-line distance), distances in this metric may be defined as:

$$d(p_i, X) = \sqrt{(p_{i1} - x_1)^2 + (p_{i2} - x_2)^2} \tag{6}$$

and the objective function of minimizing average distance as:

$$\text{minimize } z = \sum_{i=1}^{n} w_i \sqrt{(p_{i1} - x_1)^2 + (p_{i2} - x_2)^2} \tag{7}$$

In the solution methods section below, we discuss methods of finding the optimum location for each of the cases described in equations (3), (5) and (7).

B. Solution Methods

(i) In one dimension

Perhaps the simplest problem occurs when the points to be served from a location all lie along a straight line. Study the examples below and, using intuition only, estimate the location coordinate value from which the sum of the distances to the points to be served is minimum, equation (3).

Optimal Location of Facilities

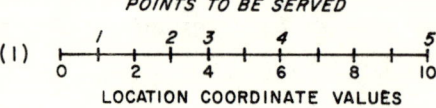

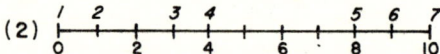

Table 2.1

Intuitive Solutions to Location Problems on a Line.

Problem	Coordinate Value
1	
2	
3	

Suppose we make a guess at the solution for problem 1 and guess a coordinate value of 5 for x. The objective function:

$$z = \sum_{i=1}^{5} |p_i - x| \quad ;$$

has the value:

$z = |1-5|+|3-5|+|4-5|+|6-5|+|10-5| = 13$

The Single-Source Location Problem

Now investigate the consequences of moving the location one unit in either direction. If it is moved to a location of 6, then all points with coordinates ≤ 5 (the previous location of x) will each contribute a one unit increase to the value of the objective function. There are three such points in this case, so the increase due to them will be three units. Conversely, all points with coordinates >6 will each contribute a one unit decrease to the value of the function. There are two such points, so the decrease due to them will be two units. The net effect, therefore, of moving the location of x from 5 to 6 is an increase in the value of the objective function from 13 to 14 units. Alternatively, a move of x from position 5 to 4 will lead to a reduction of one unit each for the first three points and an increase of one unit each for two points. The net effect is a reduction of one unit for a total distance separation of 12 units. An important generalization about all such moves can be based on this illustration: No matter where the actual locations of the points along the line are, a move from any trial source location will always lead to a decrease in the value of the objective function if it more nearly equalizes the number of points on either side of it. The limit is reached when exactly the same number of points lie on either side of the trial location. No better location can be found; this is the optimum location and is known as the _spatial_ _median_. Point (3) is the spatial median of our illustration. It is, therefore, the optimum location.

Problem 3 is different in that the points to be served sometimes share the same locations. In such cases the locations are said to be differently "weighted." The two problems shown below do not identify the points to be served by identification numbers as in the three earlier problems (notice that this information was never used). In the place of ID numbers, weights are given to be served. These might refer to numbers of people or bushels of corn. If the problem is to minimize the average distance moved by each unit, the problem is not affected by the interpretations made of the meaning of these units.

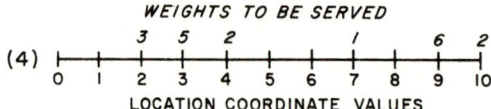

Solve problem (4) shown above. (Optimum location =   ). The principle of the median location still applies; that is, the sum of the weights on one side of the optimum location must equal the sum of the weights on the other side. The total weight involved in problem (4) is 19 units. The median is thus the tenth unit which in this case is found at a location coordinate value of 4.0.

Notice that the median location differs from the centroid of the locations. The centroid is the spatial average of the distribution.

The Single-Source Location Problem

$$\bar{x} = \sum_{i=1}^{n} (p_i/n)$$

In problem one, the centroid has the value of 4.8, a value close to our initial guess at a solution. The centroid has the property that it is the value from which the sum of the squared distances of all points is a minimum. Studies have shown that when people are asked to intuitively locate centers along a line, their guesses are usually closer to the centroid than to the spatial median even though they are attempting to find the location from which the sum of distances is least. Go back to the examples given earlier and see whether you also fell into this trap. The centroids and the median locations for these examples are given in Table 2.2 below.

Table 2.2

Correct Solutions for
the Three Problems.

Problem	Coordinate Values	
	median location	centroid location
1	4.0	4.8
2	4.0	5.0
3	2.0	3.00

The optimum point deviates in characteristic ways from the center of gravity. As we have seen, the optimum point is insensitive to the actual locations of the peripheral points. If any one of the peripheral points is moved a small amount, the center of gravity will change but the point from which the sum of the distances is minimum will not change. Because the optimum point is a median point, it will be located where the majority of points are found--this is likely to be the area of greatest density of points. Thus the optimum point favors the location of the majority and is insensitive to the locational disposition of the minority. This characteristic of the optimum point has led to the proposal of different definitions of optimality which are sensitive to the locational needs of peripherally located demand points. These definitions will be explored further in Chapter 3, Sec. 2(F).

(ii) In two dimensions

The problem of finding the optimum location for the two-dimensional case is more difficult. The case of the city-block metric will be discussed first (equation (5)). An important feature of equation (5) is that it involves the minimization of two independent variables (x_1 and x_2). Thus each can be solved separately and the contributions of each set can be added to find the total value for the objective function. When the points are arranged in a two-dimensional space, each point may be projected onto the two axes. The median point for each axis may be solved

The Single-Source Location Problem

as in the one-dimensional cases discussed earlier and the intersection of the two median lines is the optimum point sought (Fig. 2.1).

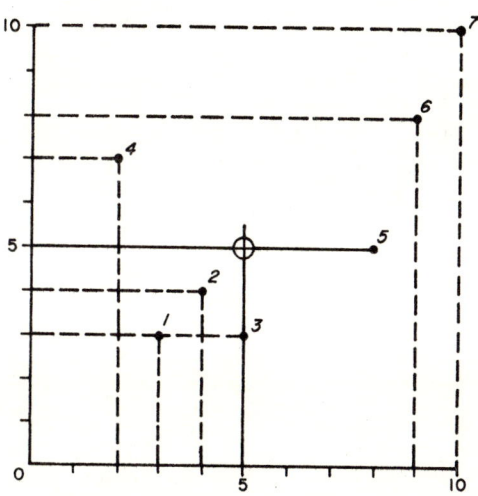

Fig. 2.1. Illustration of spatial median lines.

Solving the two-dimensional case for the euclidean metric (airline distance) is more difficult for no method is known for solving this problem directly in one analytical step. A mechanical analogue has been devised which can be used to solve simple problems. The device, known as a "Varignon Frame," consists of a board on which a map of the area to be analyzed is pasted. Holes are made through the map and board at the places corresponding to the demand points and small swivel pulleys are mounted at each hole, (Fig. 2.2). Light string is inserted over each pulley and through the holes; weights are attached to the ends proportional to the demands at the points. Above the board the strings are tied to a ring.

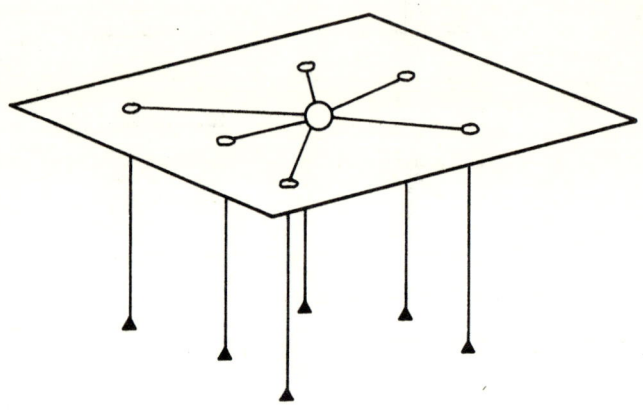

Fig. 2.2. Varignon Frame.

When the ring is allowed to find its own point of rest, that point will be the point of minimum potential energy--the point for which the average per unit distance from the demand points is least. As a device for illustrating the problem, the Varignon Frame is useful, but for most practical sized problems, it is cumbersome and inaccurate, owing to the friction of the pulleys. Accordingly, numeric-analytic techniques have been devised to solve this problem.

(iii) Exact iterative technique

The problem is solved in a series of steps (iterations) which are known always to converge on the desired optimum point. When we state in equation (7) that we wish to minimize z for the unknown location coordinates (x_1, x_2), we are stating that for any (x_1, x_2), there is a corresponding value of z. Because z is a continuous function with a single minimum point, methods of analysis which rely on moving down the gradient of this function to the low point can be used. A graph of the function z is shown in Fig. 2.3, and several sequences of iterative computational steps are shown, in all cases leading to the same optimum point.

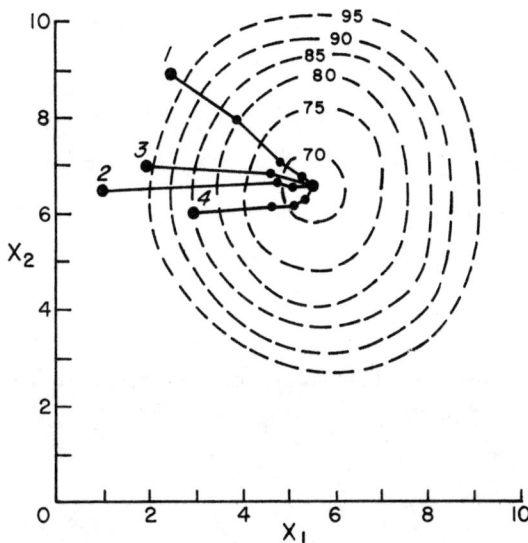

Fig. 2.3. Values of z for combinations of (x_1, x_2) and (x_1^*, x_2^*).

Table 2.3

Case Histories of Steps for
Finding Optimum Location.

	Values of z			
	Trail 1	Trail 2	Trail 3	Trail 4
Starting Location				
Computation Steps				
1				
2				
3				
4				
5				

Several writers have solved this problem by using an iterative procedure in which, starting from initial "suggested" values for the unknown coordinates of the facility location, successively more accurate values are computed. Such a procedure is often called "an algorithm"--meaning a computational strategy for accomplishing a given goal through a series of formal steps. To minimize the value z in (7), the following algorithm has been suggested (Kuhn & Kuenne, 1962).

Step 1. **Initial Location** (1) Compute the centroid.

$$x_1 = \frac{\sum_i p_{i1}}{n} \qquad (8)$$

$$x_2 = \frac{\sum_i p_{i2}}{n} \qquad (9)$$

The Single-Source Location Problem

Step 2. Find a better location for the facility.

$$x_1^* = \sum_i \frac{p_{i1}}{d(p_i,X)} \bigg/ \sum_i \frac{1}{d(p_i,X)} \qquad (10)$$

$$x_2^* = \sum_i \frac{p_{i2}}{d(p_i,X)} \bigg/ \sum_i \frac{1}{d(p_i,X)} \qquad (11)$$

where $d(p_i,X)$ is defined in equation (6).

Step 3. If the difference between x_1^* and x_1, and between x_2^* and x_2 are both less than an arbitrary small amount, terminate the algorithm; otherwise return to step 2 and recompute equations (10) and (11) using the revised values of x_1^*, x_2^* from which to compute the distances of equation (6). For succeeding values of x_1^k, x_2^k, the value of the objective function declines; (equation (7)).

A generalization for weighted demand points can be made with ease. Equations (10) and (11) become:

$$x_1^* = \sum_i \frac{p_{i1} w_i}{d(p_i,X)} \bigg/ \sum_i \frac{w_i}{d(p_i,X)} \qquad (12)$$

$$x_2^* = \sum_i \frac{p_{i2} w_i}{d(p_i,X)} \bigg/ \sum_i \frac{w_i}{d(p_i,X)} \qquad (13)$$

C. Handworked Examples

(i) The unweighted case

For a set of demand points (five in number), find the location coordinates (x_1, x_2) of a supply point such that aggregate distance separation from the supply point to each of the demand points is minimum.

Mathematical formulation (equation (7)):
Find x_1, x_2 to minimize the function:

$$z = \sum_{i=1}^{n} w_i \sqrt{(p_{i1} - x_1)^2 + (p_{i2} - x_2)^2}$$

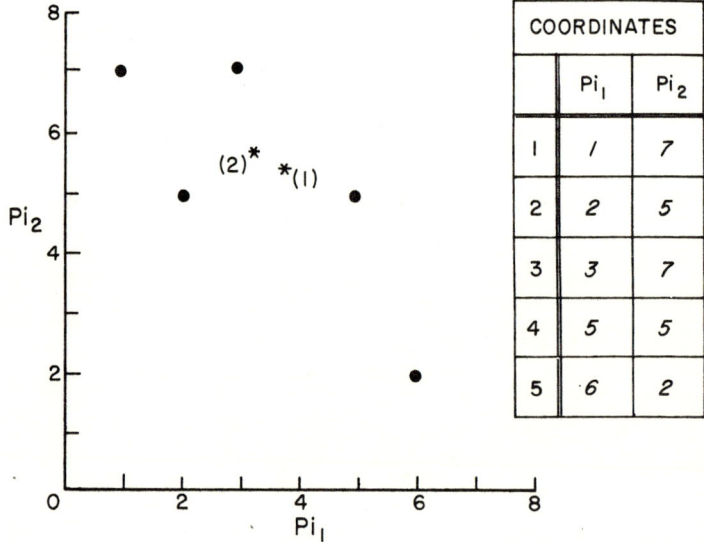

Fig. 2.4. Case study for single location problem.

The Single-Source Location Problem

1. Find initial location x_1, x_2

$$x_1 = \frac{\sum_i p_{i1}}{n} = 17/5 = 3.4 \quad \text{(from eq. 8)}$$

$$x_2 = \frac{\sum_i p_{i2}}{n} = 26/5 = 5.2 \quad \text{(from eq. 9)}$$

2. Begin iterative procedure to find a better location. See equations (10) and (11), complete the table below. Find the distance from the first point to the initial location (x_1, x_2) from equation (4).

$$d(p_1, X) = [(1 - 3.4)^2 + (7 - 5.2)^2]^{\frac{1}{2}} = 3$$

POINT	P_{i1}	P_{i2}	$1/d(p_i, X)$	$P_{i1}/d(p_i, X)$	$P_{i2}/d(p_i, X)$
1	1	7	1/3	1/3	2.33
2	2	5	0.3	1.41	3.54
3	3	7	0.7	1.63	3.80
4	5	5	0.62	3.10	3.10
5	6	2	0.24	1.46	0.48
Sum	17	26	2.44	7.93	13.25

$$x_1' = 7.93/2.44 \qquad x_2' = 13.25/2.44$$
$$x_1' = 3.24 \qquad x_2' = 5.42$$

This location is shown as (2) in Figure 2.4.

3. Return to step 2, using the new coordinates x_1', x_2' in equation (4). Terminate when changes to the source location

coordinates become small. At this point the algorithm has converged to its solution location.

(ii) The weighted case

Find facility location (x_1, x_2) to minimize distance to a set of five demand points which have unequal demands associated with them. For this problem the weighted distance separation must be minimized.

	Coordinates		Weights
	x	y	w
1	1	7	1
2	2	5	1
3	3	7	2
4	5	5	5
5	6	2	10

1. Find initial location x_1, x_2

$$x_1 = \sum_i w_i p_{i1} \Big/ \sum_i w_i = 94/19 = 4.94737$$

$$x_2 = \sum_i w_i p_{i2} \Big/ \sum_i w_i = 71/19 = 3.73684$$

(see next table) Plot this location on Figure 2.4.

The Single-Source Location Problem 57

2. Begin iterative procedure to find a better location:

$$x_1' = \sum_i \frac{w_i p_{i1}}{d(p_i,X)} \bigg/ \sum_i \frac{w_i}{d(p_i,X)}$$

$$x_2' = \sum_i \frac{w_i p_{i2}}{d(p_i,X)} \bigg/ \sum_i \frac{w_i}{d(p_i,X)}$$

Where the x point has the coordinates x_1, x_2 computed in step 1.

Complete the following table:

POINT	w_i	p_{i1}	p_{i2}	$w_i p_{i1}$	$w_i p_{i2}$	$d(p_i,X)$	$\frac{w_i p_{i1}}{d(p_i,X)}$	$\frac{w_i p_{i2}}{d(p_i,X)}$	$\frac{w_i}{d(p_i,X)}$
1	1	1	7	1	7	7.07	0.14	0.99	0.14
2	1	2	5	2	5	5.39	0.37	0.93	0.19
3	2	3	7	6	14	7.62	0.79	1.84	0.26
4	5	5	5	25	25	7.07	3.53	3.53	0.71
5	10	6	2	60	20	6.32	9.49	3.16	1.58
SUM	19			94	71		14.32	10.45	2.88

$$X_1' = 4.98; \quad X_2' = 3.63$$

Plot this location on Figure 2.4.

3. As with problem 1, return to step 2 and repeat iterations until convergence takes place.

The solution location after k iterations is:

$$x_1^k = 5.6(\pm 1); \quad x_2^k = 2.9(\pm 1) \quad .$$

In this case k is 8.

An important characteristic of the optimum point for the euclidean metric is that its location is dependent on the angular arrangements of the demand points with respect to the optimum point. If any one of these changes, the location of the optimum point will also change. Perhaps surprisingly, the distances, as such, of the peripheral demand points from the optimum point do not affect the location of the optimum point providing the angle of the demand point with respect to the optimum point is unchanged.

D. The Optimum Location in Chicago

Witzgall (1965) computed the point of minimum aggregate travel for the residential population of Chicago for both the euclidean and the city-block metrics. Data were collected for 9,600 one-quarter square mile squares covering the metropolitan area. The distribution of residences was assumed to be uniform within each grid square and thus the center of each area was used in the distance computation. The optimal location for the euclidean metric was approximately four miles west and 1.5 miles south of the Chicago central loop area. For the manhattan metric the optimal point was 0.6 miles to the east and 0.04 miles to the south of the optimal point for the euclidean metric.

The Single-Source Location Problem

E. Homework Problems

1. Find the location of minimum average distance to serve the points in the Table.

Points	Weights	Location Coordinate	
		x_1	x_2
1	1	1	2
2	5	1	4
3	3	3	1
4	10	6	6
5	4	1	3
6	2	2	6
7	5	3	5
8	8	9	7
9	9	10	8
10	10	8	9

   a) with the city-block distance metric
   b) with airline distance metric

   Answer: (a) x_1 = 2.255; x_2 = 4.486; after 10 iterations.
   (b) x_1 = 2.1673; x_2 = 4.3309; after 8 iterations.

2. (a) The unweighted case.

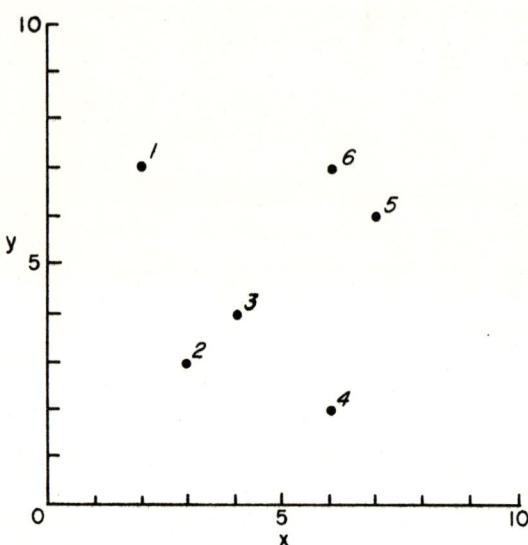

	Coordinates	
	x	y
1	2	7
2	3	3
3	4	4
4	6	2
5	7	6
6	6	7

Find the optimum location.

Answer: $x_1 = 4.437$; $x_2 = 4.459$; after 3 iterations.

(b) The weighted case: Assume the following weights are associated with the demand points.

The Single-Source Location Problem

Points	Weights
1	1
2	7
3	8
4	10
5	2
6	2

Find the optimum location.

Answer: $x_1 = 4.266$; $x_2 = 3.550$.

3. After determining the optimum location, prove with an empirical example that the location of the optimum point depends not on the length of the distances of the points from the optimum point, but only on the direction. That is, extend outward one of the peripheral points so that its angle, as seen from the optimum point, is unchanged. Then re-compute the location of the optimum point.

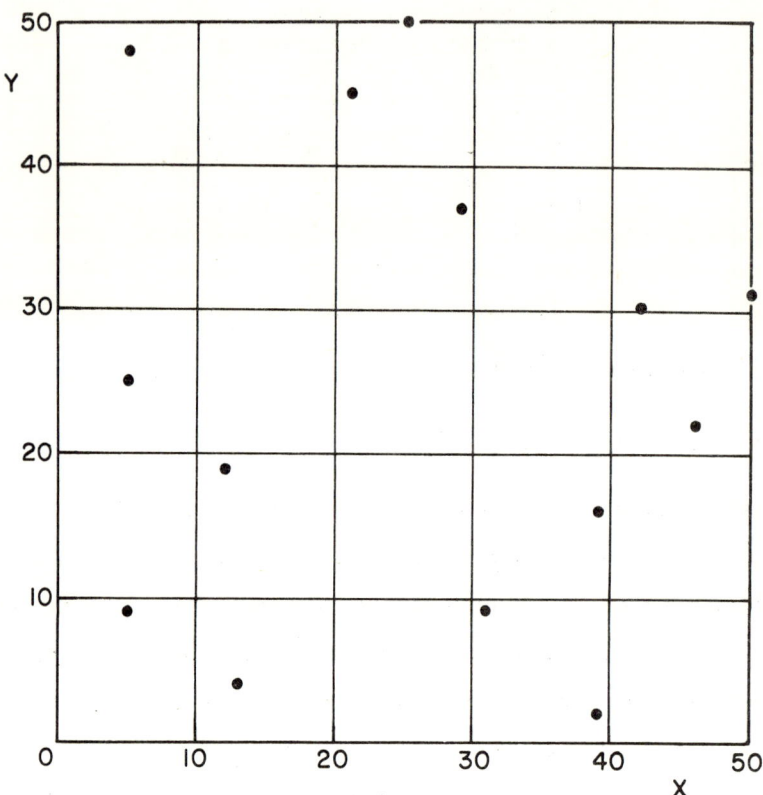

Intuitive Estimates

	X	Y	Total Distance	Index of Efficiency Equation (9)
1				
2				
3				
4				
5				
6				

Fig. 2.5a. Locate a facility to minimize total distance separation.

The Single-Source Location Problem   63

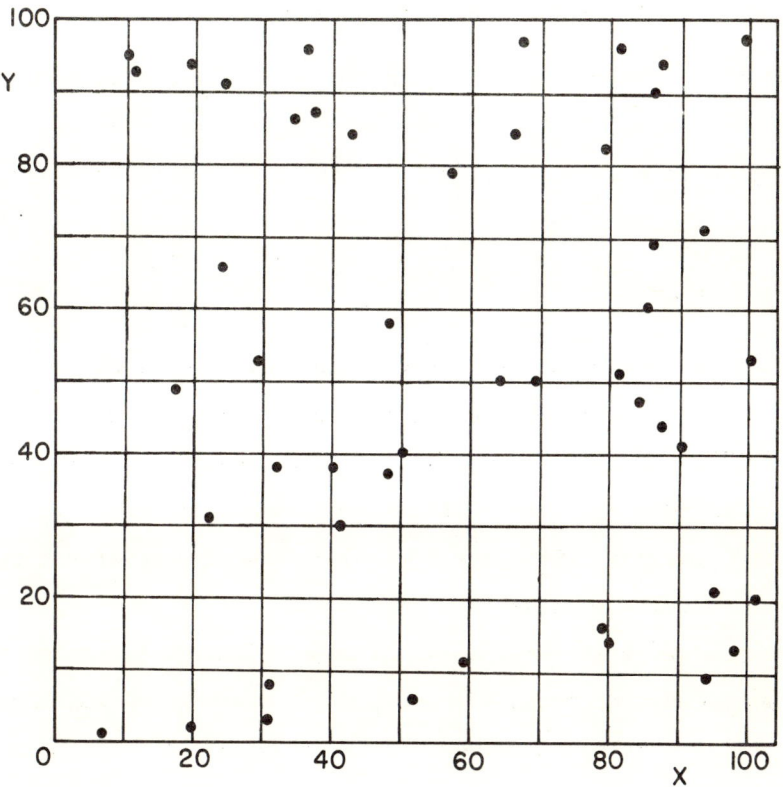

Intuitive Estimates

	X	Y	Total Distance	Index of Efficiency
1				
2				
3				
4				
5				
6				
7				
8				

Fig. 2.5b. Locate a facility to minimize total distance separation.

2. Locations on a Route Structure

When the optimum location must be found for a situation in which movement can occur only along prescribed routes on a network, methods of solution are different from those discussed earlier.

A. The Problem

Given distances defined between each node-point of a route network, find that point from which the sum of the distances to all other points is least. Weights may be associated with the nodes. The node for which this is true is called the median of the graph. Hakimi (1964) has developed a theorem showing that the desired optimum point is itself a node on the network. That is, there never will lie a point on an arc between two nodes that will have a smaller total distance to the remaining nodes than either of the nodes themselves. This is an important theorem since it has encouraged the development of solution methods which evaluate alternative nodes on the route network to find the solution node. No time needs to be spent unnecessarily examining points along the arcs connecting nodes.

Hakimi's theorem states:

> There is a point of the graph which minimizes the sum of the weighted shortest distances from all nodes to that point which is itself a node of the graph.

The Single-Source Location Problem

Define a_i = the weight attached to the ith node;

d_{ij} = the shortest distance from node i to node j;

N = the set of all nodes on the network;

r = any point on the network;

Define K = the set of nodes which reach point r most efficiently via node p (Fig. 2.6); that is

$$d_{kr} = d_{kp} + d_{pr}, \quad k \in K \tag{14}$$

Define J = the set of nodes which reach point r most efficiently via node q; that is,

$$d_{jr} = d_{jq} + d_{qr}, \quad j \in J \tag{15}$$

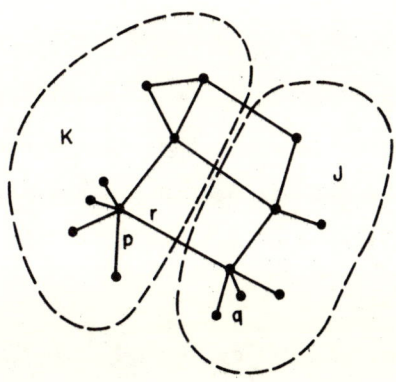

Fig. 2.6. Illustration of Hakimi's theorem.

Then the total weighted distance to the point r for the set N is the addition of the weighted distances for the two sets:

$$\sum_{i \in n} a_i d_{ir} = \sum_{k \in K} a_k (d_{kp} + d_{pr}) + \sum_{j \in J} a_j (d_{jq} + d_{qr}) \qquad (16)$$

If the sum of the weights of the nodes within the set K which focuses on node p (note no mention is made of their distances from p) is greater than the sum of the weights of the nodes in the set J, then the location r will have a larger weighted distance than location p since it will involve the larger weighted set K incurring the additional distance pr while saving the smaller weighted set K the same distance. Therefore, a larger total weighted distance would accrue to the system for this value r. This would be true of all values of r between any p,q nodes.

B. Solution Method

The optimum location can be found by inspecting the nodes. Define a distance matrix D of d_{ij} between all pairs of nodes v_i, v_j. If equal weights are attached to the nodes, then the optimum location (the network median) is that node for which the sum of the elements in the corresponding column of D is minimized. That is, let

$$d_j = \sum_{i=1}^{n} d_{ij} \qquad (j = 1, 2 \ldots, n) \qquad (17)$$

then v is the network median if and only if:

$$d_k = \min(d_1, d_2, \ldots, d_n) \qquad (18)$$

The Single-Source Location Problem

If the nodes of the network have unequal weights, then it is necessary to define a weighted-distance matrix R whose elements, r_{ij}, are the product of the node weight and the distance.

$$R = [r_{ij}] = [w_i d_{ij}] \qquad (19)$$

Each r_{ij} represents the weighted distance quantity associated with demand node v_i if v_j were the unique source for serving v_i. The network median is defined as in (17) and (18) above but over the matrix R.

C. Handworked Example

Although the solutions in the handworked examples shown below may seem intuitively self-evident, Fig. 2.7 shows a more complex network where the solution is not so clear. The difference in efficiency between node 1 and node 2 is such that if node 2 were chosen to serve this area over node 1, an approximately 10 percent increase in total distance travelled would result. Node 1 is the spatial median in this example.

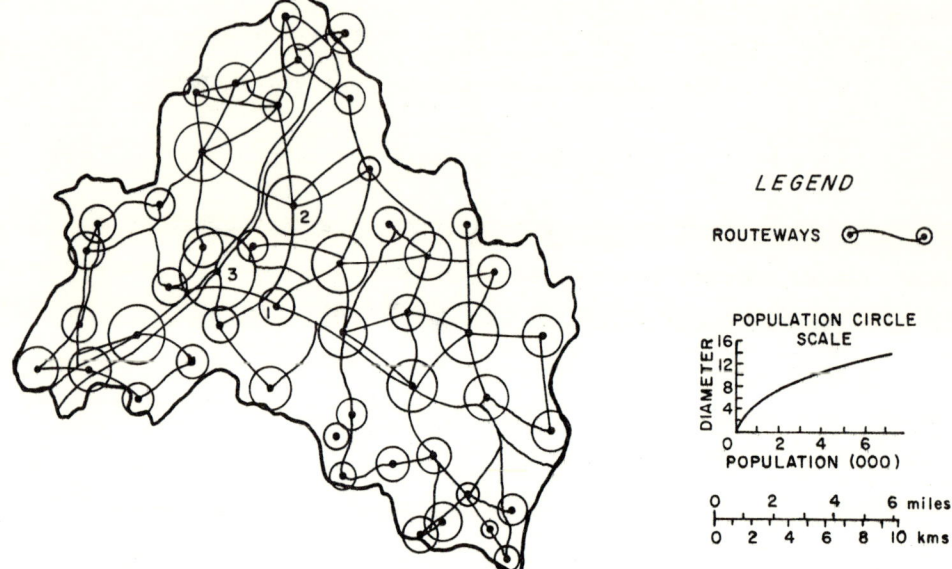

Fig. 2.7. Spatial median for weighted demands on a route structure.

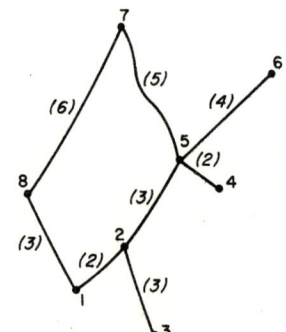

Fig. 2.8. Illustrative network.

The following table shows distances between the nodes of the map in Fig. 2.8.

	Weights w_i	Distance Matrix (D)							
		1	2	3	4	5	6	7	8
1	3	0	2	5	7	5	6	9	3
2	1	2	0	3	5	3	7	8	5
3	2	5	3	0	8	6	9	11	8
4	1	7	5	8	0	2	6	7	10
5	1	5	3	6	2	0	4	5	8
6	1	9	7	9	6	4	0	9	12
7	2	9	8	11	7	5	9	0	6
8	4	3	5	8	10	8	12	6	0

For the unweighted case the network median is the node corresponding to the minimum of the column sums of the D matrix, (equations 17 and 18). In this case node 2 and node 5 each have an aggregate distance from the remaining seven nodes of 33 units. Note how the principle of the spatial median applies to the network as it did to the plane. In the illustration there are as many nodes closer to 5 than to 2 as there are nodes closer to 2 than to 5. Changing the distances of the nodes from nodes 2 and 5 will not change this solution unless the nodes moved change their ordered relationship with nodes 2 and 5. For example, the distance from node 5 to node 6 could be shortened or lengthened without affecting the solution.

For the weighted case the weighted-distance matrix must be computed (equation (19)).

Weighted Distance Matrix (R)

	1	2	3	4	5	6	7	8
1	0	6	15	21	15	27	27	9
2	2	0	3	5	3	7	8	5
3	10	6	0	16	12	18	22	16
4	7	5	8	0	2	6	7	10
5	5	3	6	2	0	4	5	8
6	9	7	9	6	4	0	9	12
7	18	16	22	14	10	18	0	12
8	12	20	32	40	32	48	24	0
Column Totals	63	63	95	104	78	128	102	72

The column minima is the same for nodes 1 and 2. Either node would therefore serve equally well for the complete network.

D. **Program** ALLOC

Program ALLOC may be used to compute the spatial median of a network. Fig. 2.9 shows the deck setup for using this program. It will be used for several problems in Chapter 3 so the effort to master these details here will be useful then.

The Single-Source Location Problem

INPUT:

Card Set	Columns	Format	Program Name	Type	Description
DATA					
(1)	1-5	7I5	M	INT	Total Number of Places in the inter-place distance matrix
Format Statement					
(2)	1-80	20A4	FMT1	Real	Fortran format statement for one row of matrix described in 3 below
Place ID and Distance Deck					
(3)	First field as specified by user in 2 above		IJK	INT	ID number in first element of row being read in
	2nd - Mth field as specified by user in 2 above		D	INT	Interpoint Distances
Format Statement					
(4)	1-80	20A4	FMT2	Real	Fortran Format Statement for ID and Weight of each place in 5 below
Place ID's and Weights Deck					
(5)	First field as specified by user in 4 above		IKD	INT	Place ID
	2nd field as specified by user in 4 above		W	INT	Place Weight The cards may be in any order
Control Card					
(6)	1-5		MP	INT	Place 1 in col. 5
	6-10		MALG	INT	Place 1 in col. 10
(7)	Source location ID to begin with				
	1-5		JS	INT	Place ID for initial estimate

```
                            1 1 1 1 1 1 1 1 1 1 2 2 2 2 2 2 2 2 2 2 3 3 3 3 3 3
      1 2 3 4 5 6 7 8 9 0 1 2 3 4 5 6 7 8 9 0 1 2 3 4 5 6 7 8 9 0 1 2 3 4 5
1st         8
    ( I 2 , 8 I 3 )
    1         0     2       5       7       5       9       9       3
    2         2     0       3       5       3       7       8       5
    3         5     3       0       8       6       9       1       8
    4         7     5       8       0       2       6       7     1 0
    5         5     3       6       2       0       4       5       8
    6         9     7       9       6       5       0       9     1 2
    7         9     8     1 1       7       5       9       0       6
    8         3     5       8     1 0       8     1 2       6       0
    ( I 3 , I 4 )
    1           3
    3           2
    4           1
    2           1
    6           1
    5           1
    7           2
    8           4
              1         1
              4
```

Fig. 2.9. Sample input data for program ALLOC--to solve handworked example.

E. Transformation of the Distance Matrix

By transforming the distance matrix prior to analysis by the ALLOC algorithm, some different problems can be solved. Consider the following case that superficially appears to be quite different from problems discussed previously: A manufacturer wishes to set up a factory to manufacture a product. He knows the location pattern of the demand for his product but the location of his suppliers would depend on his choice of location. Different suppliers have, moreover, different prices for the supplies he needs. Imagine three potential suppliers, (Fig. 2.10).

The Single-Source Location Problem   73

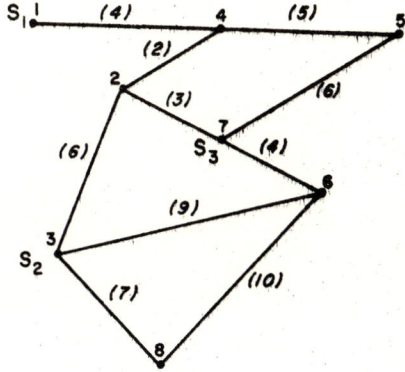

Fig. 2.10.   Route network with three possible suppliers of
             materials for a facility to be located at any node on
             the network to supply variable demands at the eight
             nodes.

This problem can be solved by regarding the three suppliers as demand points and computing one row of the weighted-distance matrix. Each element in this row would give the transport cost plus price for taking a unit to the column node (the potential facility location) from whichever supplier could deliver the unit at least total cost. Each element of this row is then added to the weighted distance element in the same column for the demand point whose location coincides with the least cost supplier. The procedure is listed as a series of steps that are then illustrated with a handworked example.

Step 1.   Determine distances from potential suppliers to potential facility locations.

Step 2. Determine the least cost supplier to each potential facility location node. Least cost means cost of the material plus cost of transporting it to the potential facility location.

Step 3. Determine the transfer cost to each potential facility location for the quantity of product required at those demand points whose locations coincide with the potential facility locations.

Step 4. Add the product delivery transfer costs in step 3 to the supply costs for the minimum-cost supply centers.

Step 5. Incorporate the inter-point interaction costs in step 4 in the original inter-point distance matrix.

Handworked example of the transformation process.

Step 1. Per-unit transport costs between nodes.

		Weight w_i	Supplier Price per unit	Potential Facility Locations							
				1	2	3	4	5	6	7	8
Possible Suppliers	1	20	40	0	6	12	4	9	13	9	19
	2	20	45	12	6	0	8	13	9	9	7
	3	20	45	9	3	9	5	6	4	0	14
Demand Points	1	5		0	6	12	4	9	13	9	19
	2	4		6	0	6	2	7	7	3	13
	3	9		12	6	0	8	13	9	9	7
	4	2		4	2	8	0	5	9	5	15
	5	1		9	7	13	5	0	10	6	20
	6	3		13	7	9	9	10	0	4	10
	7	6		9	3	9	5	6	4	0	14
	8	4		19	13	7	15	20	10	14	0

The Single-Source Location Problem 75

Step 2. Transport costs of assembling materials from the three potential suppliers $(w_i d_{ij})$.

Cost of Material $(w_i p_i)$	Potential Facility Locations							
	1	2	3	4	5	6	7	8
1 800	0	120	240	80	180	260	180	380
2 900	240	120	0	160	260	180	180	140
3 900	180	60	180	100	120	80	0	280

Total cost at potential facility locations from suppliers. $(w_i p_i + w_i d_{ij})$

	1	2	3	4	5	6	7	8
1 (1)	800	920	1040	880	980	1060	980	1180
2 (3)	1140	1020	900	1060	1160	1080	1080	1040
3 (7)	1080	960	1080	1000	1020	980	900	1180
Minimum	800	920	900	880	980	980	900	1040

Step 3. Transport costs for delivering product to the demand points located at the supply centers.

	w_i	1	2	3	4	5	6	7	8
1 (1)	5	0	30	60	20	45	65	45	95
2 (3)	9	108	54	0	72	117	81	81	63
3 (7)	6	54	18	54	30	36	24	0	92

Step 4. Total interaction costs for assembling materials and distributing product for the potential supply sites.

		1	2	3	4	5	6	7	8
Demand	1	800	950	60	900	1025	65	45	95
Points	3	108	54	900	72	117	81	81	1103
	7	54	18	54	30	36	1004	900	92

Step 5. Transformed data input for the alternating or vertex substitution algorithms.

			Potential Facility Locations						
	w_i	1	2	3	4	5	6	7	8
	1	1	800	950	60	900	1025	65	45	95
	2	4	6	0	6	2	7	7	3	13
	3	1	108	54	900	72	117	81	81	1103
	4	2	4	2	8	0	5	9	5	15
	5	1	9	7	13	5	0	10	6	20
Demand	6	3	13	7	9	9	10	0	4	10
Points	7	1	54	18	54	30	36	1004	900	92
	8	4	19	13	7	15	20	10	14	0

F. Homework Problems

1. Suppose an increase of one unit weight is made to each node in the previous example, would the spatial median be affected?

2. Suppose there were a proportional increase in the weights of all nodes in the previous example, would the spatial median be affected?

3. Code the network shown here and find the node that minimizes the distances to the other nodes. (Distances are in parentheses.)

The Single-Source Location Problem

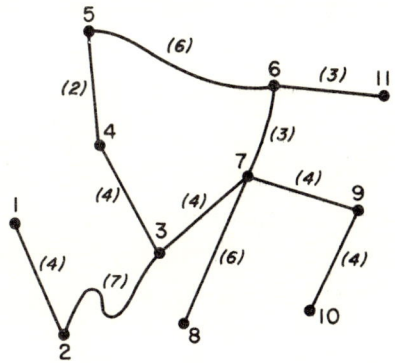

	Weights
1	10
2	8
3	2
4	2
5	6
6	8
7	2
8	3
9	10
10	4
11	4

4. You are an electrical contractor who specializes in the maintenance of electrical equipment in the recreational centers of the White Mountains of New Hampshire. When a facility requires service, it calls you and you have promised to respond immediately. a) You wish to select a location in the area from which your average response time will be least. A table of driving times between the facilities is shown below.

APPROXIMATE MINUTES OF DRIVING TIME TO ATTRACTIONS

WHERE YOU ARE / THE PLACE YOU WISH TO VISIT	A.M.C. HEADQUARTERS	CLARK'S TRADING POST	FRANCONIA NOTCH STATE PARK	CRAWFORD NOTCH STATE PARK	LOON MOUNTAIN	LOST RIVER RESERVATION	MT. CRANMORE SKIMOBILE	MT. WASHINGTON AUTO ROAD	NATURELAND	POLAR CAVES	SANTA'S VILLAGE	SIX GUN CITY	STORY LAND	WILDCAT MT. GONDOLAS
A.M.C. HEADQUARTERS	–	89	74	40	93	101	30	6	86	127	46	38	18	2
CLARK'S TRADING POST	89	–	15	53	5	12	67	83	3	38	54	51	73	87
FRANCONIA NOTCH STATE PARK	74	15	–	38	20	27	72	68	12	53	39	36	60	72
CRAWFORD NOTCH STATE PARK	40	53	38	–	58	65	34	46	50	91	45	42	22	42
LOON MOUNTAIN	93	5	20	58	–	15	62	88	8	41	59	56	68	91
LOST RIVER RESERVATION	101	12	27	65	15	–	77	95	15	46	66	63	83	99
MT CRANMORE SKIMOBILE	30	67	72	34	62	77	–	36	70	103	76	68	12	32
MT WASHINGTON AUTO ROAD	6	83	68	46	88	95	36	–	80	121	40	32	24	4
NATURELAND	86	3	12	50	8	15	70	80	–	41	51	48	72	84
POLAR CAVES	127	38	53	91	41	46	103	121	41	–	92	89	109	125
SANTA'S VILLAGE	46	54	39	45	59	66	76	40	51	92	–	8	64	44
SIX GUN CITY	38	51	36	42	56	63	68	32	48	89	8	..	56	36
STORY LAND	18	73	60	22	68	83	12	24	72	109	54	56	–	20
WILDCAT MT. GONDOLAS	2	87	72	42	91	99	32	4	84	125	44	36	20	–

Source: White Mountains Recreation Association, Vacation Guide, 1973.

b) Suppose you decided to locate so that your longest travel time from any of the facilities would be least. Where would you locate?

5. a) Complete the analysis for the handworked example "transformation of the distance matrix" determining which is the second-best location for the proposed factory. Which supplier would be used?

b) Rank the locations in order of their desirability for being the home of the proposed factory.

Answers: Qu. 1. Yes, node 2 would become the unambiguous spatial median.
Qu. 2. No
Qu. 3. ?????
Qu. 4a) ?????
4b) Franconia Notch State Park
Qu. 5a) Node 2 using supplier 1 (Total cost 1106);
b) 4,1;2,1;1,1;3,2;7,3;6,3;5,1;8,2

Chapter 3 - Multi-Facility Location in Continuous Space

The location problem in most cases involves either the simultaneous or the sequential location of many facilities. In either case the best location for any one facility depends on the locations of the others in the system. Solving the problem of the location of many facilities in a system involves many of the principles developed in Chapter 2 as well as several new ones. As before, we can distinguish between location on a continuous plane and location on a network of routes.

A. The Problem

Suppose we have n demand points to be supplied at minimum cost by m supply centers. Where should the m centers be located? Notice the objective function is the same as in Chapter 2; that is, we need to minimize average unit distance from the demand points to their closest supply point. In Chapter 2 it was unnecessary to specify the closest supply point since only one such point was involved. In the multi-facility case the demand points are clustered in partitions around their respective supply centers. Figure 3.1 illustrates a solution to one problem; the partitions are indicated as are the total distances that have been minimized. One important characteristic of this and all solutions to this problem is that the location of each source is optimum with respect to the points in its partition.

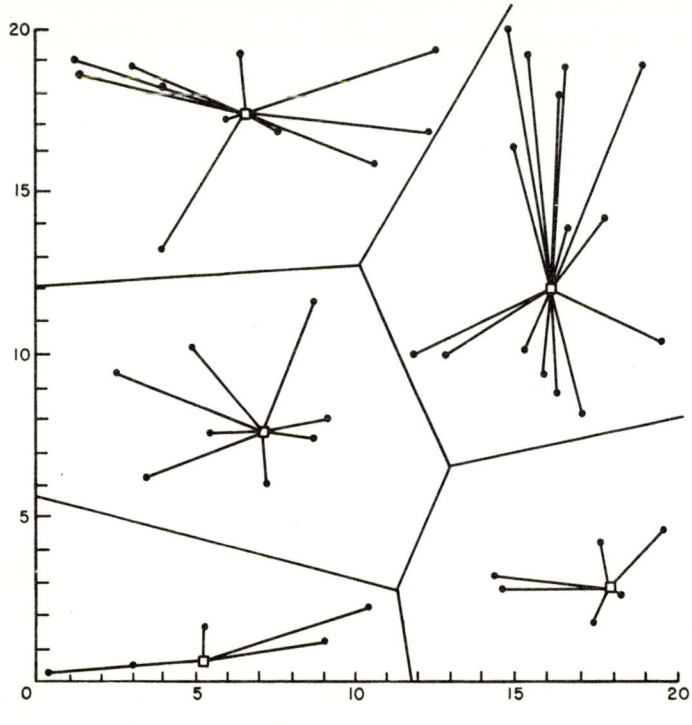

●–WEIGHTED DEMAND POINTS
□–SOURCE LOCATIONS

Fig. 3.1. The multi-facility location problem on the plane. Source: Unpublished paper by James A Kohler.

(Data for this illustration is homework problem #1B.)

A mathematical formulation of the distances shown by lines in Fig. 3.1 is:

$$z = \sum_{i=1}^{n} \sum_{j=1}^{m} a_{ij} w_i \sqrt{(x_i - x_j)^2 + (y_i - y_j)^2} \qquad (20)$$

where:

z is the aggregate distance from all demand points to their closest supply center.

x_i, y_i are the corrdinates of the ith demand point (i = 1,...,n).

x_j, y_j are the coordinates of the jth supply center (j = 1,...,m).

w_i is the weight assigned to the ith demand point.

a_{ij} = 1 when demand point i is served from supply center j, otherwise a = 0.

B. <u>Solution Methods</u>

   (i) Intuitive

We might first consider how well multi-facility location problems can be solved by human intuition since that is how such problems are commonly solved. Figure 3.2 shows 15 demand points for which the best locations for 3 supply centers are needed. Record your estimates for these locations (x_j, y_j) for evaluation by the Instructor's Program.

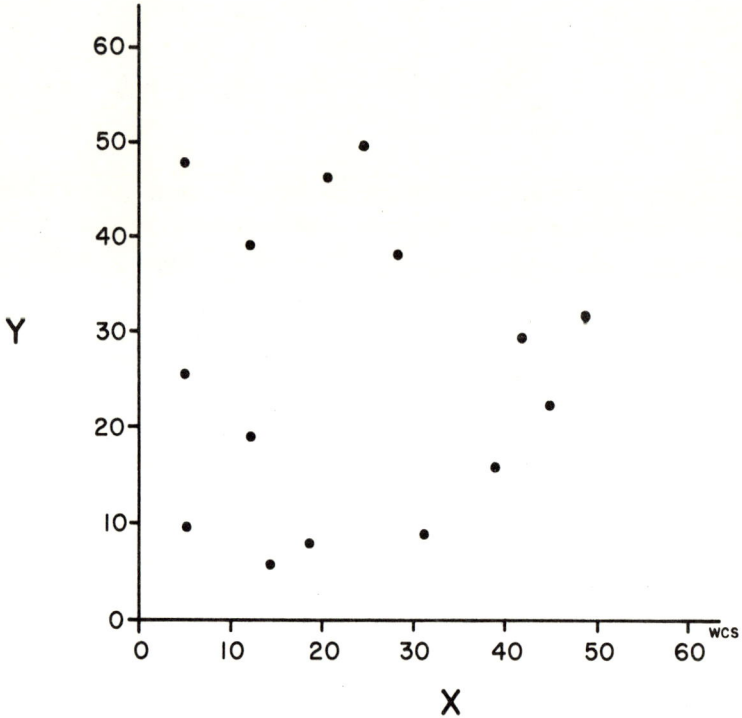

Fig. 3.2. Sample Problem.

Multi-Facility Location in Continuous Space 83

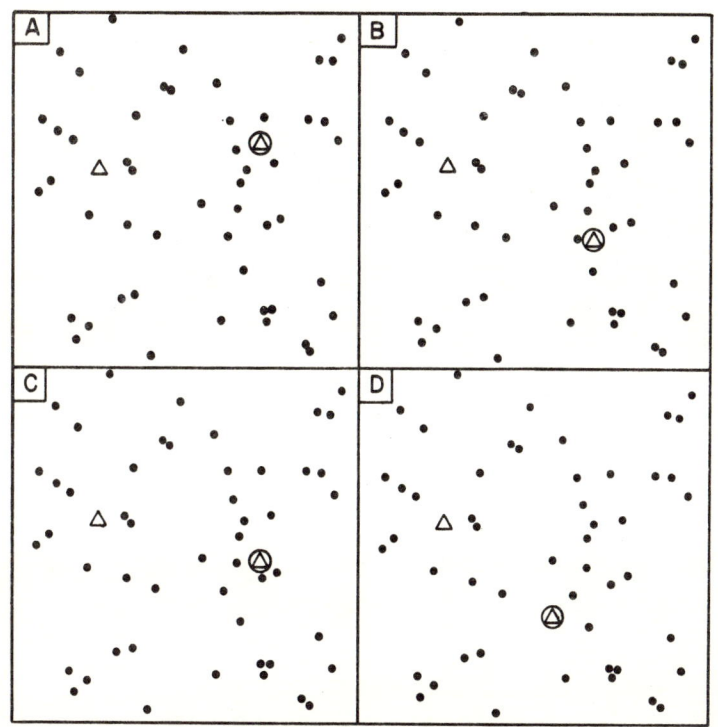

△ FIXED FACILITY LOCATION
◬ VARIABLE FACILITY LOCATION

Fig. 3.3. Paired-comparisons of solutions for the two-facility case. Source: Developed from data in S. Eilon et al., 1971, p. 67.

Reproduced by permission of the publishers, Charles Griffin & Company Ltd. of London and High Wycombe, from Eilon, Watson-Gandy and Christofides DISTRIBUTION MANAGEMENT, 1971.

Paired Comparisons tableaux

Indicate with a 1 in each cell in which the column solution is better than the row solution-otherwise, 0.

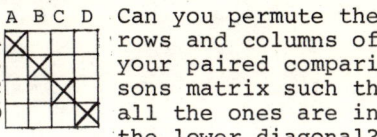

Can you permute the rows and columns of your paired comparisons matrix such that all the ones are in the lower diagonal?

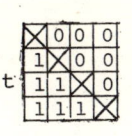

Paired Comparisons of Solutions. In Figure 3.3 a series of comparisons between alternative "solutions" to a multi-facility location problem are made. On this map one facility is always located in the same place. The location of the other varies from one case to another. Complete the paired comparisons tableau in Table 3.1 indicating which solution you think is closer to the optimum solution in terms of the value of the objective function. One of the four possibilities is the optimum solution, the others represent 3.3%, 7.3% and 11.7% increases in the value of the objective function, respectively. As problems become more complex, the efficiency of solutions derived from human intuition declines. Numerical techniques at this point must take over the task of finding adequate solutions.

(ii) The alternating heuristic algorithm

This algorithm is developed from the principle noted in the previous discussion of the problem that the solution to the multi-facility case involves partitions (groups) of the demand points with each facility located best with respect to its group. For any group, therefore, the problem reduces to finding the solution for the single-facility case. As we noted in Chapter 2, an exact solution to this problem is available through the use of the iterative equations. In the multi-facility case the problem remaining is, then, to find the partitions. The alternating algorithm starts with partitions surrounding arbitrary facility locations. After finding the optimum locations within each group, it then redefines the groups around the new locations and finds new center locations for these new groups. We will show that at every step the value of the objective function z decreases--until stability occurs. The algorithm is a heuristic and unlike the methods discussed in Chapter 2, it cannot guarantee that the best solution will always be found. Indeed, if the algorithm is repeated on the same set of data starting with different center locations, the results may be better or worse than other runs of the algorithm. The number of iterations required before stability occurs is few. This has become, therefore, the most popular computerized algorithm to compute a large problem. It is common for researchers using this algorithm to compute a large number of solutions from different starting locations and to select the locations with the smallest value of the objective function as the desired optimum locations.

Step 1. Select starting locations for the centers;

Step 2. Form groups of demand points by allocating each demand point to it's closest center, calculate z (eq. (20));

$$z = \sum_{i=1}^{n} \sum_{j=1}^{m} a_{ij} w_i \sqrt{(x_i - x_j)^2 + (y_i - y_j)^2}$$

x_i, y_i demand point coordinates i = 1,n(13)

x_j, y_j supply point coordinates j = 1,m(3)

a_{ij} = 1 when demand point i is closest to supply center j; otherwise 0.

Step 3. Calculate new center locations by solving the single-facility location problem for each group of demand points:

$$x_j^* = \sum_{i=1}^{n} \frac{a_{ij} w_i x_i}{d_{ij}} \bigg/ \sum_{i=1}^{n} \frac{a_{ij} w_i}{d_{ij}} \qquad y_j^* = \sum_{i=1}^{n} \frac{a_{ij} w_i y_i}{d_{ij}} \bigg/ \sum_{i=1}^{n} \frac{a_{ij} w_i}{d_{ij}}$$

Step 4. Go to Step 2 and repeat until there is no change in the value of z.

In Fig. 3.4 convergence of the algorithm is illustrated for a different set of starting locations than in the worked example that follows.

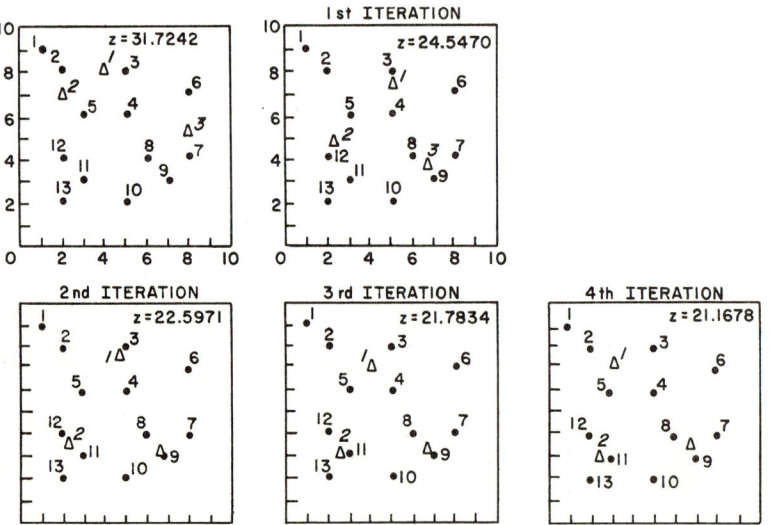

Fig. 3.4. Convergence of the alternating algorithm.

Multi-Facility Location in Continuous Space

C. Handworked Example

For a set of thirteen weighted demand points find the location of three supply centers such that the aggregate distance of the units from the demand points to their nearest supply center is minimum (eq. (20)).

For the first problem, weights are unity.

demand point	location coordinates		weights problem #		demand point	location coordinates		weights problem #	
	x_i	y_i	1	2		x_i	y_i	1	2
1	1	9	1	2	8	6	4	1	8
2	2	8	1	2	9	7	3	1	8
3	5	8	1	3	10	5	2	1	7
4	5	6	1	3	11	3	3	1	3
5	3	6	1	2	12	2	4	1	3
6	8	7	1	10	13	2	2	1	8
7	8	4	1	10					

First Iteration

Step 1. Select starting center locations (arbitrary).

	x_j	y_j
1	1	1
2	8	2
3	8	8

Step 2. Form groups of demand points by allocating to closest supply center.

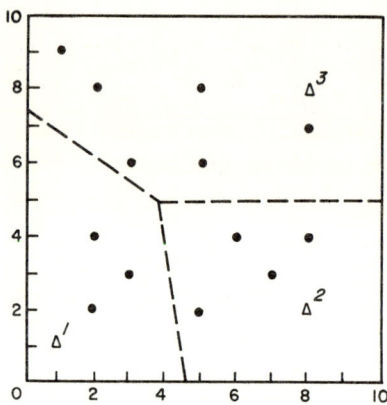

Fig. 3.5. Assignment of the demand points to their closest source.

Step 3. Organize computation table by groups of allocated demand points. Solve the one center point of minimum aggregate travel for each group.

Multi-Facility Location in Continuous Space

Group assigned to center 1.

1 demand point	2 closest center a_{ij}	3 location coordinates x_i	y_i	4 d_{ij}	5 $\dfrac{a_{ij}w_ix_i}{d}$	6 $\dfrac{a_{ij}w_i}{d_{ij}}$	7 $\dfrac{a_{ij}w_iy_i}{d_{ij}}$	8 supply center location x_j^*	y_j^*
First iteration for this group.									
11	1	3	3	2.828	1.061	.354	1.06	1.0	1.0
12	1	2	4	3.162	.632	.316	1.265		
13	1	2	2	1.414	1.414	.707	1.414		
Sums				7.405	3.107	1.377	3.740		
Second iteration for this group.									
11	1	3	3	.796	3.771	1.257	3.771	2.257	2.716
12	1	2	4	1.309	1.528	.764	3.055		
13	1	2	2	.761	2.629	1.315	2.629		
Sums				2.866	7.927	3.335	9.455		
Third iteration for this group.									
11	1	3	3	.645	4.654	1.551	4.654	2.377	2.835
12	1	2	4	1.225	1.633	.817	3.266		
13	1	2	2	.916	2.183	1.092	2.183		
Sums				2.785	8.470	3.460	10.104		
Fourth iteration for this group.									
11	1	3	3	.557	5.383	1.794	5.383	2.448	2.920
12	1	2	4	1.169	1.711	.855	3.422		
13	1	2	2	1.024	1.953	.977	1.953		
Sums				2.750	9.047	3.626	10.758		

After 8 iterations, the optimum location for this group x_j^*, y_j^* is: 2.554, 2.998.

Group assigned to center 2.

First iteration for this group.

1	2	3	4	5	6	7	8
7	2	8	4	2.0	4.0	0.5	2.0	8.0	2.0
8	2	6	4	2.828	2.121	0.354	1.414		
9	2	7	3	1.414	4.950	0.707	2.121		
10	2	5	2	3.0	1.667	0.333	0.667		
Sums				9.243	12.738	1.894	6.202		

Second iteration for this group.

1	2	3	4	5	6	7	8
7	2	8	4	1.467	5.455	0.682	2.727	6.725	3.275
8	2	6	4	1.026	5.849	0.975	3.900		
9	2	7	3	0.388	18.021	2.574	7.723		
10	2	5	2	2.145	2.331	0.466	0.932		
Sums				5.025	31.656	4.697	15.282		

After three iterations, the optimum location for this group is:
$x_j^* = 6.739$ and $y_j^* = 3.253$.

Group assigned to center 3.

First iteration for this group.

1	2	3	4	5	6	7	8
1	3	1	9	7.071	0.141	0.141	1.272	8.0	8.0
2	3	2	8	6.0	0.333	0.167	1.333		
3	3	5	8	3.0	1.667	0.333	2.667		
4	3	5	6	3.606	1.387	0.277	1.664		
5	3	3	6	5.385	0.557	0.186	1.114		
6	3	8	7	1.0	8.0	1.0	7.0		
Sums				26.062	12.085	2.104	15.051		

Iterations for this group	x*	y*
1	5.742	7.152
2	4.680	7.167
3	4.365	7.194
4	4.211	7.190
5	4.123	7.179
6	4.072	7.172
7	4.040	7.160

Second Iteration

Form groups of demand points by allocating to the closest supply center (as computed in the first iteration). See diagram.

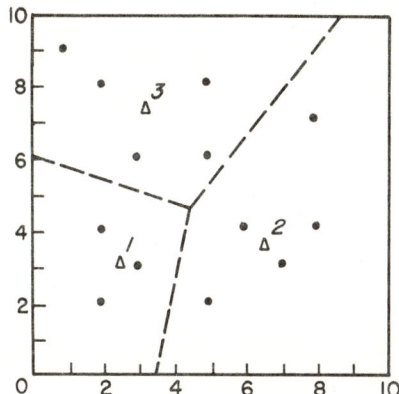

Note that the demand point with coordinates 8,7 is now assigned to the group surrounding the second center. In this second iteration, the optimum locations for the second and third centers are changed to reflect these new assignments. In the table describing computations for the second iteration, the computations for the first cycle only of the iterative algorithm are shown. Below the computations for each subgroup, the coordinates for subsequent iterations for the subgroup are shown. The iterations were terminated in this case when the coordinates for both x_j^* and y_j^* changed less than 0.05 in the previous iteration.

Optimal Location of Facilities

1	2	3		4	5	6	7	8	
demand point	closest center	location coordinates		d_{ij}	$\dfrac{a_{ij}w_i x_i}{d_{ij}}$	$\dfrac{a_{ij}w_i}{d_{ij}}$	$\dfrac{a_{ij}w_i y_i}{d_{ij}}$	supply center locations	
		x_i	y_i					x^*_j	y^*_j
11	1	3	3	.506	5.925	1.975	5.925	2.495	2.967
12	1	2	4	1.146	1.746	0.873	3.491		
13	1	2	2	1.086	1.842	0.921	1.842		
Sums				2.738	9.513	3.769	11.258		
Subsequent iterations								2.524	2.987
								2.542	2.995
								2.554	2.998
Second group									
6	2	8	7	3.953	2.024	0.253	1.771	6.739	3.254
7	2	8	4	1.465	5.460	0.682	2.730		
8	2	6	4	1.051	5.711	0.952	3.808		
9	2	7	3	0.364	19.246	2.749	8.248		
10	2	5	2	2.144	2.332	0.466	0.933		
Sums				8.977	34.773	5.103	17.489		
Subsequent iterations								6.814	3.427
								6.816	3.519
								6.806	3.576
								6.795	3.609
Third group									
1	3	1	9	3.551	0.282	0.282	2.535	4.040	7.166
2	3	2	8	2.204	0.907	0.454	3.629		
3	3	5	8	1.271	3.933	0.787	6.29		
4	3	5	6	1.510	3.311	0.6622	3.973		
5	3	3	6	1.562	1.920	0.640	3.840		
Sums				10.099	10.352	2.824	20.269		
Subsequent iterations								3.666	7.178
								3.446	7.177
								3.323	7.185
								3.257	7.197
								3.221	7.210

The total weighted distance after the second iteration

$$z = 21.1678$$

Third Iteration

The assignment of demand points to centers is unchanged. The solution locations are:

Supply Center	x	y
1	2.56827	3.00013
2	6.77763	3.64126
3	3.18118	7.23443

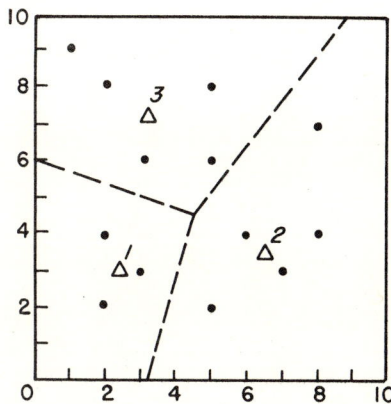

Fig. 3.6. Solution supply center locations after <u>3</u> iterations of the alternating algorithm.

Total weighted distance after the third iteration

$$z = 21.1679$$

Second Problem

This problem has the same demand point locations as the first problem but different weights to be served are now assigned to these points. The weights are given in the initial data table for the first problem. Fig. 3.4 shows the convergence process for this problem. The computations for the first iteration are given in the tableau below. Notice the addition of column 4b to this tableau. The objective function z is the sum of the sums in this column.

First Iteration.

Starting Locations:

	x_j	y_j
1	7	8
2	5	5
3	6	2

1	2	3		4	4b	5	6	7	8	
demand point	closest center	location coordinates				$a_{ij}w_ix_i$	$a_{ij}w_i$	$a_{ij}w_iy_i$	supply center location	
point	$a_{ij}=1$	x_i	y_i	d_{ij}	w_id_{ij}	d_{ij}	d_{ij}	d_{ij}	x_j'	y_j'
3	1	5	8	3.16065	9.48195	4.74586	.949172	7.59338	7.99845	7.00052
6	1	8	7	.001629	.0162918	49104.4	6138.05	42,966.3		
Sums				3.16228	9.49824	49109.1	6139.00	42,973.9		
1	2	1	9	5.35662	10.7132	.373369	.373369	3.36033	4.37115	4.83754
2	2	2	8	3.9529	7.9058	1.01192	.505958	4.04766		
4	2	5	6	1.32146	3.964737	11.3511	2.27022	13.6213		
5	2	3	6	1.79791	3.59581	3.33722	1.11241	6.67443		
8	2	6	4	1.83121	14.6496	26.2122	4.36871	17.4748		
11	2	3	3	2.29297	6.87892	3.92503	1.30834	3.92503		
12	2	2	4	2.5151	7.54531	2.38559	1.19279	4.77117		
Sums				19.0682	55.2531	48.5965	11.1318	53.8448		
7	3	8	4	1.44876	14.4876	55.2196	6.90245	27.6098	6.93484	3.01799
9	3	7	3	.0676	.5408	828.402	118.343	355.029		
10	3	5	2	2.1863	15.3041	16.0088	3.20176	6.40351		
13	3	2	2	5.03874	40.31	3.17539	1.5877	3.17539		
Sums				8.7414	70.6425	902.806	130.035	392.218		
Sums				30.9719	135.394	50060.5	6280.16	43420.00		

Multi-Facility Location in Continuous Space

Table 3.2

Computation for Second Problem.

Alternating Algorithm iterations	Iterations to find location for each group	Total Weighted Distance z	Locations of Supply Centers 1		2		3		Supply Center	Weighted Distance for Group	IDs of Demand Points Assigned
			x^*_j	y^*_j	x^*_j	y^*_j	x^*_j	y^*_j			
1	1	154.249	7.0	8.0	4.683	4.838	5.875	2.700	1	20.142	3,6
	2		7.475	7.175	4.545	4.808	6.027	2.777			
	3		7.821	7.060	4.419	4.812	6.173	2.844			
	4		7.944	7.019	4.424	4.821	6.306	2.899			
	5		7.983	7.006			6.426	2.943	2	55.509	1,2,4,5, 8,11,12
	6						6.530	2.977			
	7						6.618	3.000			
	8						6.690	3.015			
	9						6.748	3.024	7	78.598	7,9,10,13
	10	136.008					6.795	3.028			
2	1	123.08	7.994	7.002	3.001	4.563	6.878	3.172	1	9.613	3,6
	2				2.595	4.161	6.894	3.193			
	3				2.439	3.895					
	4				2.375	3.779			2	70.808	1,2,4,5,11 12,13
	5				2.362	3.729					
	6	104.33			2.367	3.700			3	41.664	7,8,9,10
3	1	102.27	7.997	7.000	2.231	3.555	6.895	3.194	1	19.000	3,4,6
					2.227	3.482	6.895	3.203			
					2.239	3.425			2	42.516	1,2,5,11, 12,13
		101.80			2.250	3.378			3	40.756	7,8,9,10
4	1	101.71	8.000	7.000	2.259	3.341	6.893	3.209			No change in Assignments

Note the changes in assignments after the first and second iterations.

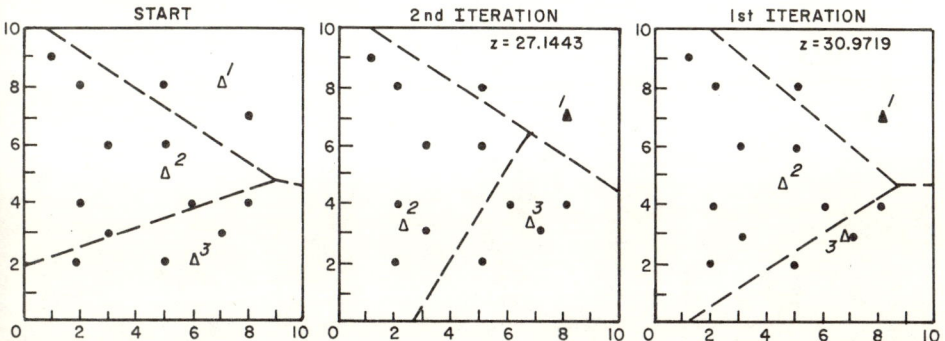

Fig. 3.7. Convergence for alternating algorithm for second problem.

D. **Programs for this Problem**

   (i) Program ALTERN

Though the alternating algorithm is simple, it is computationally laborious and realistically sized problems cannot be solved by hand calculations in a reasonable length of time. Program ALTERN, written by L. A. Ostresh, does these calculations and iterates until convergence occurs.

INPUT REQUIREMENTS

    (1) PROGRAM ALTERN

    (2) Title card

    (3) Control card

    (4) Data cards

(1) Program ALTERN - this may be a source deck in FORTRAN; an object deck, or system control cards to a program library.

(2) Title card - any title anywhere in the eighty columns.

(3) Control card   cols.

Number of demand points	1-5
Number of supply sources	6-10
Input format for location coordinates and weights for demand point data	21-80

(4) Data cards. Each data card must contain two locational coordinates (x ,y). If weights are not unity the location coordinates must be followed in each case by the appropriate weight. Punch decimal points.

Multi-Facility Location in Continuous Space

EXAMPLE INPUT

The data below is that for problem two of the handworked examples.

Columns of data cards

```
1st  1 2 3 4 5 6 7 8 9 0 1 2 3 4 5 6 7 8 9 0 1 2 3 4 5 6 7 8 9 0
2nd  D A T A   F O R   P R O B L E M   T W O
     1 3             3                     ( 3 D 5 . 0 , I 5 )
     1 .             9 .           2 .
     2 .             8 .           2 .
     5 .             8 .           3 .
     5 .             6 .           3 .
     3 .             6 .           2 .
     8 .             7 .         1 0 .
     8 .             4 .         1 0 .
     6 .             4 .           8 .
     7 .             3 .           8 .
     5 .             2 .           7 .
     3 .             3 .           3 .
     2 .             4 .           3 .
     2 .             2 .           8 .
```

(ii) Program TORN--A step-search algorithm

The alternating algorithm is only one of several heuristic algorithms for solving the problem we have discussed. We describe below the STEP-SEARCH algorithm devised by Törnqvist and improved by Kohler (see references) to illustrate the variety of solution methods. Like the alternating algorithm, the step-search algorithm begins with an arbitrary selection of source locations. It then relocates the centers by systematically moving them one at a time, holding constant the locations of the remaining centers. This relocation proceeds in a definite pattern of trial and error steps. When the trial leads to a reduction in the value of z then a relocation takes place, otherwise the center remains in its previous location. The trial moves consist of steps taken in each of the four directions from a point according to a pre-selected length. If the objective function is reduced on any one of these steps, a further step in the same direction is made. This process continues until z no longer is reduced. At this point the size of the step is halved and trial moves are made in all directions from the relocated point. When the size of this step becomes less than a predetermined value, the movement process begins again with a new source location. Thus source locations are moved consecutively to new locations and when all sources have been evaluated once, the process is repeated. In fact, iterations of complete cycles are made until no further moves of any points take place.

Program TORN uses the step search prodecure for determining the optimum locations of a set of facilities. It was written by J. A. Kohler.

>   Maximum number of demand points, 100
>   Maximum number of supply centers, 20

In addition to using a different locational algorithm, program TORN differs from program ALTERN in that initial supply centers are input and constraints can be added to force some of the center locations to stay at fixed locations. This ability to analyze initial supply centers is useful in evaluating a set of locations and comparing their efficiency with the optimum locations.

Multi-Facility Location in Continuous Space   99

INPUT REQUIREMENTS

    -1. Program TORN

    -2. Two control cards

    -3. Data Cards

    -4. Three control cards

    -5. Initial source locations

(1) Program TORN - this may be a FORTRAN source deck, an object deck, or system control cards.

(2) Control cards

    (1) Number of problems
    (2) Number of demand points

(3) Data cards--one card for each demand point   cols.

x coordinate	punch decimal point	1-10
y coordinate	punch decimal point	11-20
w weight	punch decimal point	21-30

(4) Control cards   cols.

    (1) If next problem is for new demand data, put 1, otherwise, leave blank card here   1-5

    (2) Title card--any title here   1-80

    (3) Number of supply centers   1- 5
        Minimum step size is 1/this integer number   6-10
        Maximum step size (punch decimal point)   11-15

(5) Starting source locations, one card per source

x coordinate	punch decimal point	1-10
y coordinate	punch decimal point	11-20
Constraint-put 1 in col. 30 if this source is fixed		21-30

EXAMPLE INPUT FOR PROGRAM TORN

```
                    1 1 1 1 1 1 1 1 1 1 2 2 2 2 2 2 2 2 2 2 3
  1 2 3 4 5 6 7 8 9 0 1 2 3 4 5 6 7 8 9 0 1 2 3 4 5 6 7 8 9 0
1st         1
2nd         1 3
                    1 .           9 .                   2 .
                    2 .           8 .                   2 .
                    5 .           8 .                   3 .
                    5 .           6 .                   3 .
                    3 .           6 .                   2 .
                    8 .           7 .                 1 0 .
                    8 .           4 .                 1 0 .
                    6 .           4 .                   8 .
                    7 .           3 .                   8 .
                    5 .           2 .                   7 .
                    3 .           3 .                   3 .
                    2 .           4 .                   3 .
                    2 .           2 .                   8 .

  Blank card here
  D A T A   F O R   P R O B L E M   T W O
            3       5 0       1 . 5
                    7 .           8 .
                    5 .           5 .
                    6 .           2 .
```

E. Homework Problems

1. Use Program ALTERN to compute the optimal solutions to the problems in Figures 3.2 and 3.3. Find locations of supply points and the value of the objective function.

(a) Data for Figure 3.2.

demand points	coordinates x_i	y_i	demand points	coordinates x_i	y_i	demand points	coordinates x_i	y_i
1	5	9	6	13	39	11	39	2
2	5	25	7	28	37	12	39	16
3	5	48	8	21	45	13	45	22
4	13	4	9	25	50	14	41	30
5	12	19	10	31	9	15	49	31

(b) Data for Figure 3.3.

demand points	coordinates x_i	y_i	demand points	coordinates x_i	y_i	demand points	coordinates x_i	y_i
1	1.33	8.89	18	3.13	1.92	35	6.37	7.02
2	1.89	0.77	19	8.86	8.74	36	7.23	7.05
3	9.27	1.49	20	4.18	3.74	37	1.68	6.45
4	9.46	9.36	21	2.22	4.35	38	3.54	7.06
5	9.20	8.69	22	0.88	7.02	39	7.67	4.17
6	7.43	1.61	23	8.53	7.04	40	2.20	1.12
7	6.08	1.34	24	6.49	6.22	41	3.57	1.99
8	5.57	4.60	25	4.53	7.87	42	7.34	1.38
9	6.70	2.77	26	4.46	7.91	43	6.58	4.49
10	8.99	2.45	27	2.83	9.88	44	5.00	9.00
11	8.93	7.00	28	3.39	5.65	45	6.63	5.23
12	8.60	0.53	29	0.75	4.98	46	5.89	8.06
13	4.01	0.31	30	7.55	5.79	47	1.13	5.25
14	3.34	4.01	31	8.45	0.69	48	1.90	8.35
15	6.75	5.57	32	3.33	5.78	49	1.74	1.37
16	7.36	4.03	33	6.27	3.66	50	9.39	6.44
17	1.24	6.69	34	7.31	1.61			

Source: S. Eilon et al., 1971; see references.

Reproduced by permission of the publishers, Charles Griffin & Company Ltd. of London and High Wycombe, from Eilon, Watson-Gandy and Christofides DISTRIBUTION MANAGEMENT, 1971.

2. Data is reproduced on the following page for the 100 largest cities in the U.S.A. Prepare it for analysis by program ALTERN and compute the best five locations for serving these 100 largest cities. Latitudes and longitudes were computed to tenths of a degree and expressed in minutes. The populations of the places were "normalized", that is, each was expressed as a proportion of the total population of the 100 places. (Note: for this problem, assume that these coordinates are Cartesian coordinates.)

Table 3.3

100 MOST POPULOUS URBAN AREAS IN CONTIGUOUS
UNITED STATES, 1960, WITH LATITUDES AND
LONGITUDES IN MINUTES, AND NORMALIZED
POPULATION WEIGHTS

Set	Urban Area Centering On	North Latitude a_j	West Longitude b_j	Weight w_j
1	1. New York	2424.00'	4410.00'	0.1680
	2. Los Angeles	2040.00	7089.00	0.0772
	3. Chicago	2490.00	5247.00	0.0709
	4. Philadelphia	2400.00	4506.00	0.0433
	5. Detroit	2533.80	4893.00	0.0421
	6. San Francisco	2247.00	7336.20	0.0289
	7. Boston	2544.00	4263.00	0.0287
	8. Washington, D.C.	2313.00	4620.00	0.0215
	9. Pittsburgh	2415.60	4800.00	0.0215
	10. Cleveland	2478.00	4888.20	0.0212
2	11. St. Louis	2304.00	5409.00	0.0198
	12. Baltimore	2350.80	4582.80	0.0169
	13. Minneapolis	2700.00	5589.00	0.0164
	14. Milwaukee	2581.80	5253.60	0.0137
	15. Houston	1767.00	5715.00	0.0136
	16. Buffalo	2551.20	4713.00	0.0125
	17. Cincinnati	2346.00	5058.00	0.0118
	18. Dallas	1948.20	5788.20	0.0111
	19. Kansas City	2341.20	5659.80	0.0110
	20. Seattle	2841.00	7332.00	0.0103
3	21. Miami	1527.00	4809.00	0.0101
	22. New Orleans	1800.00	5401.80	0.0101
	23. San Diego	1947.00	7026.00	0.0100

Source: Kuenne, Robert and Richard M. Soland. The Multisource Weber Problem. Arlington, Va.: IDA, 1971, p. 20-23.

Table 3.3 (continued)

Set	Urban Area Centering On	North Latitude a_j	West Longitude b_j	Weight w_j
3	24. Denver	2367.00	6300.00	0.0100
	25. Atlanta	2007.00	5053.80	0.0091
	26. Providence	2490.00	4275.00	0.0078
	27. Portland	2719.20	7344.00	0.0078
	28. San Antonio	1755.00	5898.00	0.0076
	29. Indianapolis	2367.00	5166.00	0.0076
	30. Columbus	2375.40	4081.80	0.0073
4	31. Louisville	2299.80	5128.80	0.0072
	32. San Jose	2232.00	7293.00	0.0072
	33. Phoenix	1998.00	6721.80	0.0066
	34. Memphis	2106.00	5400.00	0.0065
	35. Birmingham	1998.00	5193.00	0.0062
	36. Norfolk	2192.40	4570.80	0.0060
	37. Fort Worth	1947.00	5832.00	0.0060
	38. Dayton	2367.00	5046.00	0.0060
	39. Rochester	2587.20	4642.20	0.0059
	40. Akron	2462.40	4878.60	0.0055
5	41. Albany	2544.00	4409.40	0.0054
	42. Sacramento	2299.20	7278.00	0.0054
	43. Springfield,Mass.	2524.20	4341.00	0.0054
	44. Toledo	2484.00	5001.00	0.0052
	45. Oklahoma City	2116.80	5839.80	0.0051
	46. Omaha	2649.00	5760.00	0.0046
	47. Hartford	2487.00	4345.20	0.0045
	48. San Bernardino	2044.20	7030.80	0.0045
	49. Youngstown	2463.00	4824.00	0.0044
	50. Jacksonville,Fla.	1812.00	4884.00	0.0044
6	51. Bridgeport	2467.20	4387.20	0.0044
	52. Salt Lake City	2427.00	6693.00	0.0041
	53. Nashville	2166.00	5190.00	0.0041

Table 3.3 (continued)

Set	Urban Area Centering On	North Latitude a_j	West Longitude b_j	Weight w_j
6	54. Richmond	2240.40	4636.20	0.0040
	55. Syracuse	2581.80	4566.00	0.0040
	56. St. Petersburg	1647.00	4944.00	0.0039
	57. Ft. Lauderdale	1564.80	4804.80	0.0038
	58. Tampa	1654.80	4942.80	0.0036
	59. Tulsa	2164.20	5734.80	0.0036
	60. Grand Rapids	2554.20	5134.00	0.0035
7	61. Wichita	2245.80	5832.00	0.0035
	62. Wilmington	2367.60	4518.60	0.0034
	63. New Haven	2470.80	4353.00	0.0033
	64. Flint	2581.80	5004.00	0.0033
	65. El Paso	1887.00	6387.00	0.0033
	66. Mobile	1824.00	5283.00	0.0032
	67. Allentown	2422.00	4518.00	0.0030
	68. Trenton	2409.00	4465.80	0.0029
	69. Albuquerque	2103.00	6382.80	0.0029
	70. Des Moines	2481.00	5601.00	0.0029
8	71. Wilkes-Barre	2469.00	4530.00	0.0028
	72. Tuscon	1929.00	6634.20	0.0027
	73. Davenport	2479.20	5421.60	0.0027
	74. Spokane	2844.00	7032.60	0.0027
	75. Worcester	2530.20	4288.80	0.0027
	76. South Bend	2484.00	5169.00	0.0026
	77. Tacoma	2829.60	7338.00	0.0026
	78. Canton	2428.80	4873.80	0.0025
	79. Fresno	2184.60	7168.20	0.0025
	80. Scranton	2475.00	4524.00	0.0025
9	81. Charlotte, N.C.	2101.80	4830.00	0.0025
	82. Harrisburg	2410.20	4592.40	0.0025
	83. Newport News	2195.40	4575.60	0.0025
	84. Shreveport	1938.00	5607.60	0.0025

Table 3.3 (continued)

Set	Urban Area Centering On	North Latitude a_j	West Longitude b_j	Weight w_j
9	85. Chattanooga	2101.20	5110.80	0.0024
	86. Orlando	1699.80	4872.60	0.0024
	87. Baton Rouge	1818.00	5466.00	0.0023
	88. Utiea	2583.60	4509.00	0.0022
	89. Austin	1810.80	5848.20	0.0022
	90. Pomona	2042.40	7047.00	0.0022
10	91. Little Rock	2064.20	5530.20	0.0022
	92. Peoria	2425.80	5362.80	0.0022
	93. Ft. Wayne	2463.00	5104.80	0.0021
	94. Erie	2524.20	4803.00	0.0021
	95. Corpus Christi	1648.20	5835.60	0.0021
	96. W. Palm Beach	1585.20	4803.00	0.0021
	97. Knoxville	2160.00	5014.20	0.0021
	98. Rockford	2529.60	5343.60	0.0020
	99. Savannah	1922.40	4864.20	0.0020
	100. Charleston	2293.80	4884.00	0.0020
				100.1400

Multi-Facility Location in Continuous Space

3. Select a map of the city, district or state of your choice which shows the areas for which population census statistics are tabulated. (See United States Census of Population, 1970 or the censuses of other countries.) Lay a fine-grid of graph paper over the map and assign Cartesian coordinates to the approximate centers of each administrative unit. Solve the facility location problem for the one source and multi-source location problem.

Answers to homework problem 1 and Table 3.1.

Problem	Fig.	Number of Centers	Location Coordinates						Value of z equation (1)	Coefficient of Efficiency
			x_j	y_j	x_j	y_j	x_j	y_j		
1	3.2	1								
2	3.2	2								
3	3.2	3	8.888	14.466	20.997	44.998	40.361	17.968	143.209	1.0
4	3.3	1	5.62	4.90					180.128	1.0
5	3.3	2	2.67	5.65	7.24	4.54			135.522	1.0
6	3.3	3	2.33	5.15	7.40	1.65	7.06	6.84	105.214	1.0
7	3.3	4	3.13 7.35	1.92 6.22	2.46	7.05	7.43	1.61	84.154	1.0
8	3.3	5	3.13 8.63	1.92 7.52	7.44 6.66	1.58 5.21	2.46	7.05	72.238	1.0

Answers to exercise in Fig. 3.3.

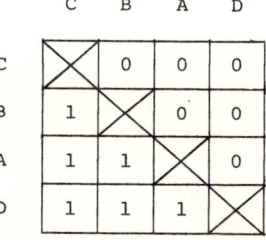

Chapter 4 - Multi-Facility Location on a Network

(1) Minimizing Average Distance

A. The Problem

As with the case for the continuous plane, multi-facility location problems on a network can be regarded as a generalization of the single facility case. In this section we will solve the problem when average distance is to be minimized, then consider the other objective functions discussed in chapter one and discuss solution methods for them. We will show that most of these problems can be solved using program ALLOC by manipulating three control cards.

For the problem of minimizing average distance, as with the single source case, Hakimi's theorem still holds that a solution to this problem exists with the locations at nodes of the network. This property of the solution allows us to investigate the demand nodes as potential locations for the supply centers and to ignore all other locations that are not nodes on the network knowing that we are not ignoring locations that would be better solutions.

Mathematical Formulation

$$\text{minimize } z = \sum_{i=1}^{n} \sum_{j=1}^{m} a_{ij} w_{ij} d_{ij} \qquad (21)$$

where a = 1 when demand point i is closer to supply point j than to any other supply center; otherwise 0. w_i = weight of demand point i; d_{ij} = shortest distance between demand points i and j. Notice from the above formulation that one way of interpreting the problem is "choose m demand points from n demand points to be the supply centers for the remaining n-m demand points." Whereas in the continuous plane cases, supply centers could occur at new locations, in the network case we are choosing the best locations from the n demand point sites.

B. Solution Methods

(i) Intuitive

Many practical location problems belong to the category being considered here yet, surprisingly little is known about the characteristics of problems that can be solved moderately well by human intuition and those that are generally solved poorly by this method. No doubt the reason is that until recently it was impossible to know whether a problem had been solved well or

Multi-Facility Location on a Network

poorly, except in the sense that someone might show that the problem could be solved more efficiently. Then the measure of the difference between the two solutions would be the measure of how well the problem had been solved in the first instance. This approach does beg the question of objective verification since the fact that no one has solved a particular problem better than a given case is no real proof of how well it has been solved. The extent of human capability and variability can be gauged in any student group by comparing performances of solutions to a problem set. A special instructor's program has been written to facilitate this (Program INTPMED). For example, Fig. 4.1 shows places with circles proportional in size to populations, a route structure and ID's for the places; Fig. 4.2 shows the route structure used in computing shortest distances between places. Complete the table which asks for identification of the best five and ten places in which to locate facilities such that average distance traveled to the closest facility would be minimum.

Number of centers to be located		ID's of places for the 3 selections
1	1	
2	5	
3	10	

After completing your own solutions to these problems, try comparing other proposed solutions to these problems in Figs. 4.2 and 4.3. What are the characteristics of problems that make some easier to solve than others? We may guess that ease and accuracy of intuitive solutions depend on the size of the problem; that is, the total number of nodes in the network; the ratio of the number of supply centers to demand points; the shape of the study area and the complexity of the connectivity of the network. All of these factors can be regarded as forces making intuitive solutions easier or more difficult in any given instance. Since we don't know how any one of these forces truly affects human ability in this area, the result of the combination of all operating at once is unknown to us. We surely require methods of solution whose accuracy is known and unrelated to the vagaries of the shape and complexity of the study area.

Multi-Facility Location on a Network

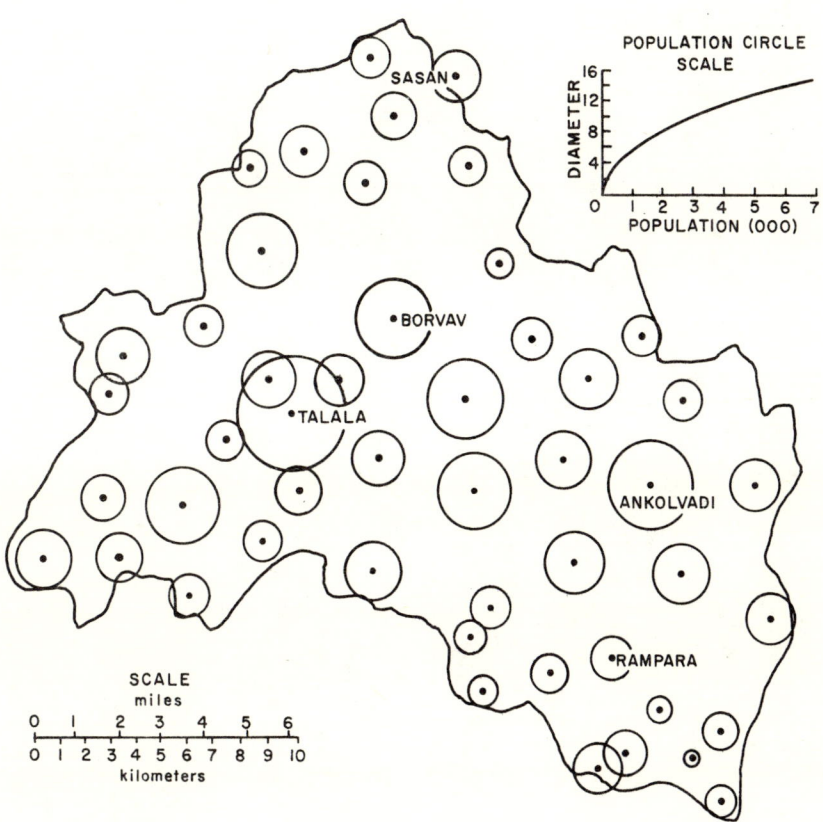

Fig. 4.1.

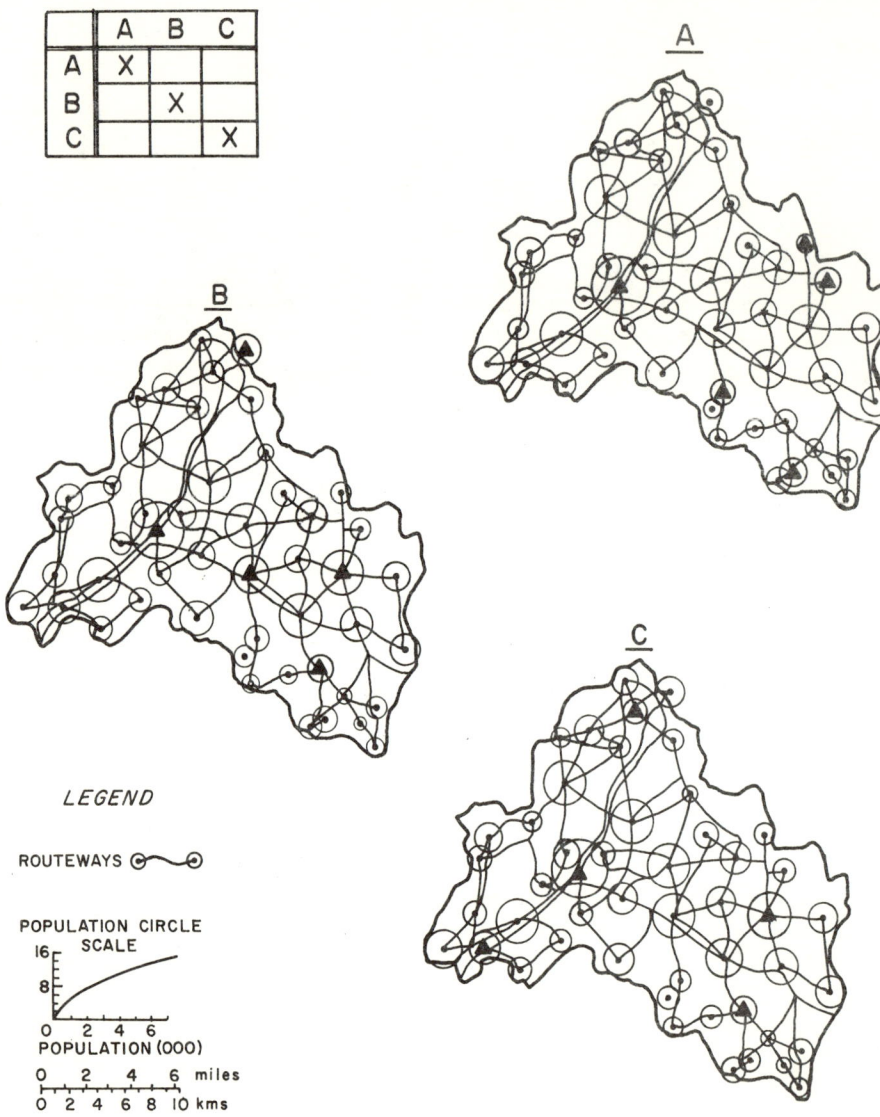

Fig. 4.2. Paired comparisons of five center solutions.

Is map A a more efficient solution than map B?

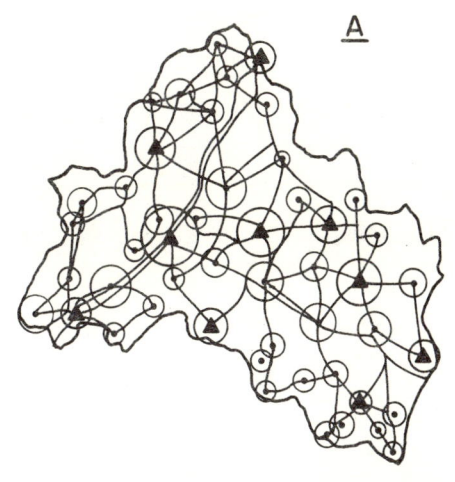

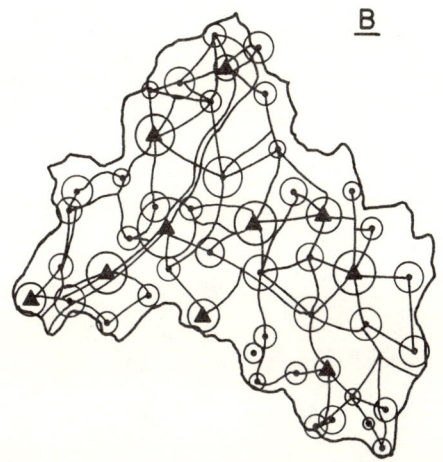

Fig. 4.3. Paired comparisons of ten center solutions.

(ii) Numerical

In this section we will describe two heuristic algorithms for solving the problem of finding locations for a set of points to minimize their average distance from a set of weighted demand points.

<u>The</u> <u>alternating</u> <u>heuristic</u>. This algorithm, originally devised by Maranzana (1964), follows the same principles as the alternating heuristic for the continuous plane. As in that case, it uses to advantage the knowledge that a property of the solution sought is that all the demand points closest to a particular supply center should be arranged such that the supply center is the point of minimum average distance to them. This should be true of all supply centers. The algorithm is described as a series of steps.

Assume n demand points and m supply centers.

Step 1. Select m demand points as the starting locations of the m supply centers.

Step 2. Allocate the demand points to their closest supply centers and compute the value of the objective function z (eq. (1)).

Step 3. Find the optimum location for each group of demand points identified in the allocation process in Step 2. Use method for single-source location on a route structure (2.2).

Step 4. Repeat Step 2, allocating demand points to the supply centers identified in Step 3, calculate z. If the groups of demand points have changed, continue; otherwise terminate.

The vertex-substitution heuristic. This algorithm, developed by Teitz and Bart (1968), operates on the principle of making single-node substitutions of nodes not in the supply-center set for nodes in the set when it can be shown that the value of the objective function z will thereby decrease. The algorithm is described as a series of steps.

Step 1. Select m demand points as the starting locations of the m supply centers.

Step 2. Take a demand point not within the supply center set and substitute it in turn for each of the supply centers. Make the substitution permanent for the supply center (if any) that leads to the greatest decline in the value of z (removing from the set the supply center for which it was substituted).

Step 3. Repeat step 2 for all demand points.

Step 4. Call steps 2 and 3 a complete cycle. If a complete cycle has led to no permanent substitutions, terminate; otherwise return to step 2 and start a new cycle.

Comparison of the algorithms. In comparing any two algorithms which have been designed to solve the same problem a number of criteria are relevant: accuracy, robustness, speed, efficiency and problem size.

(1) Accuracy. Accuracy means the likelihood in any problem of finding the true minimum of the objective function or of being close to it. The alternating class of algorithms have the characteristic that they terminate on reaching a "stable partition" of the demand points. A stable partition is any spatial grouping of demand points, such that each group is served by a supply center that minimizes average distance with respect to the group; and all members of the group are closer to the supply center than to any other supply center. As soon as an algorithm of this kind reaches a stable partition, it terminates. Yet, it is known that there exist stable partitions for most problems that have higher values of z than other stable partitions. When an algorithm terminates in one of the poorer stable partitions, it is said to have reached a "local minimum" instead of the "global minimum" that it is seeking. Kohler (1973) identified five different stable partitions in fifty trial runs from different starting locations for a problem with 50 demand points and three supply centers in a continuous plane case. For five centers he identified 14 stable partitions and for ten centers 50 stable partitions. It seems that as

the number of centers increases, so increases the number of stable partitions (and the likelihood of becoming trapped in a local minima situation). Typically, the response to this problem is either to introduce some perturbation to the supply center locations when a stable partition is found and see whether a lower value of the objective function is found, or simply repeat the algorithm many times accepting the best value found as the solution desired. There is, however, no certainty that even then the best solution has been found. Some experimenters have compared the best solution obtained with such heuristic algorithms with solutions obtained by enumerating all possible groupings of the demand points. This approach may sound attractive but in practice becomes impractical even for small problems. For a two center problem with twenty demand points, there are 524,287 different allocations of the points to the centers while with four centers and twenty demand points, there are 45,232,115,901 different allocations! Even for modern computers these are large numbers requiring many hours of computer time to evaluate.

Repeated runs of the alternating algorithm (Maranzana) for a five center problem and forty-nine demand points (starting with a random selection of centers) gave a range of solutions (stable partitions) that are shown in Fig. 4.4. The same number of runs were made for the same problem using the vertex substitution algorithm (Teitz and Bart), and in every case the solution was the same with a value of the objective function less than the smallest ever found with the alternating algorithm. Care must be taken in making a generalization about the relative accuracy of the two algorithms on the basis of inductive evidence such as this, but in fact more evidence is available on the vertex substitution algorithm outperforming the alternating one. The reason for this is related to the earlier discussion of stable partitions where we saw that the alternating class of algorithms became trapped in such sub-optimal solutions. The vertex substitution algorithm has no such similar weakness.

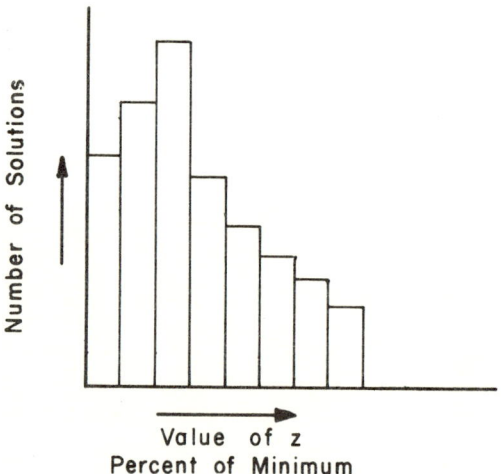

(2) <u>Robustness</u>. Robustness means the reliability of an algorithm to perform well in a variety of situations.

Knowledge of the robustness can be accumulated by examining performance statistics as they become available, or expectations on robustness can be inferred from a few well-chosen experiments in which the range of properties that characterize problems are systematically varied. Further conclusions on robustness can be made from knowledge of how the algorithm is logically organized. It is frequently possible to predict the circumstances in which that logic might perform less well. We have already seen how the number of stable partitions increases as the number of demand points and centers increase, and we can, therefore, anticipate that the reliability of these algorithms declines as these parameters of the problem studied increase. From the logic of the vertex substitution algorithm, we can conclude that no simple exchange of points will ever be missed by the algorithm. Rather, only in cases where two or more centers must simultaneously be exchanged for demand points not previously selected to effect a decrease in the value of the objective function, will the optimum point be missed. Such circumstances do not appear to be related to problem size which leads to the expectation that this algorithm is more robust than the alternating one over ranges of problem sizes.

(3) <u>Speed-Cost</u>. Different algorithms require different amounts of computer time to solve the same problem and the ratio

between costs is not constant for all problem sizes. Thus the vertex substitution algorithm requires twice as much time as the alternating algorithm for a 50 x 5 problem and more than twice the amount for larger problems. In the same amount of computer time needed for one solution of the vertex substitution algorithm, the alternating algorithm can compute several independent solutions to a problem.

C. Handworked Examples

(i) The alternating (Maranzana) algorithm

Problem: For the ten weighted node network in Fig. 4.5, find the two centers from which the weighted distances of the demand points to their closest center is minimum. The first computation involves finding the shortest paths between all pairs of demand points. We will discuss this problem formally in Chapter 5. This example is sufficiently simple for these distances to be found by visual inspection.

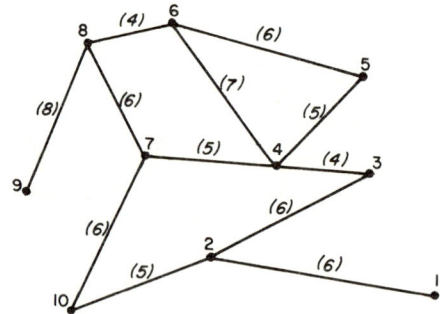

Fig. 4.5. Network for handworked example.

Multi-Facility Location on a Network

	w_i	1	2	3	4	5	6	7	8	9	10
1	4	0/0	6/24	12/48	16/64	21/84	23/92	17/68	23/92	31/124	11/44
2	1	6/6	0/0	6/6	10/10	15/15	17/17	11/11	17/17	25/25	5/5
3	3	12/36	6/18	0/0	4/12	9/27	11/33	9/27	15/45	23/69	11/33
4	1	16/48	10/30	4/12	0/0	5/15	7/21	5/15	11/33	19/57	11/33
5	1	21/21	15/15	9/9	5/5	0/0	6/6	10/10	10/10	18/18	16/16
6	4	23/92	17/68	11/44	7/28	6/24	0/0	10/40	4/16	12/48	16/64
7	2	17/34	11/22	9/18	5/10	10/20	10/20	0/0	6/12	14/28	6/12
8	1	23/23	17/17	15/15	11/11	10/10	4/4	6/6	0/0	8/8	12/12
9	2	31/62	25/50	23/46	19/38	18/36	12/24	14/28	8/16	0/0	20/40
10	1	11/11	5/5	11/11	11/11	16/16	16/16	6/6	12/12	20/20	0/0

Step 1. Select initial supply centers (arbitrary choice). In this case choose nodes 2 and 5.

Step 2. Partition the demand points among the two centers. Row demand point is allocated to column center corresponding to cell with row minima. The sum of the row minima is therefore the value of the objective function z.

$$z = \sum_{i=1}^{10} \sum_{j=1}^{2} a_{ij} w_i d_{ij}$$
$$= 152$$

	2	5	row min.
1	$\underline{24}$	84	24
2	$\underline{0}$	15	0
3	$\underline{18}$	27	18
4	$\underline{30}$	$\underline{15}$	15
5	15	$\underline{0}$	0
6	68	$\underline{24}$	24
7	22	$\underline{20}$	20
8	17	$\underline{10}$	10
9	50	$\underline{36}$	36
10	$\underline{5}$	16	5
Sum			152

Step 3. Find the optimum location for each partition.

Node 2 subset

	1	2	3	10
1	0	24	48	44
2	6	0	6	5
3	36	18	0	33
10	11	5	11	0
Sums	53	◇47◇	65	82

Node 5 subset

	4	5	6	7	8	9
4	0	15	21	15	33	57
5	5	0	6	10	10	18
6	28	24	0	40	16	48
7	10	20	20	0	12	28
8	11	10	4	6	0	8
9	38	36	24	28	16	0
Sums	92	105	◇75◇	99	87	159

Column minima of node 2 subset is node 2(47).

Column minima of node 5 subset is node 6(75).

Therefore substitute node 6 for node 5 and return to step 2.

Second Iteration

Step 2.

$Z = 122$ for nodes 2 and 6

	2	6	row min.
1	24	92	24
2	0	17	0
3	18	33	18
4	30	21	21
5	15	6	6
6	68	0	0
7	22	20	20
8	17	4	4
9	50	24	24
10	5	16	5
Sum			122

Examine the partitions in the table. Are the new groups of demand points different from previous groups? No! Nodes 1, 2, 3 and 10 form one group and the remaining points comprise the second group. From the first iteration we know that the optimum locations for these groups are nodes 2 and 6. This

Multi-Facility Location on a Network 125

is therefore a stable partition in the system centered on these nodes.

(ii) The vertex substitution (Teitz and Bart) algorithm.

Problem: Same problem as for the alternating algorithm (Fig. 4.5). After computing the weighted distance matrix:

$$R = [r_{ij}] = [w_i d_{ij}]$$

Step 1. Select initial supply centers. As before we will choose nodes 2 and 5.

Step 2. Take a demand point not a supply center and substitute it for each of the supply centers in turn.

Supply Centers				Substitute node 1 for				Substitute node 1 for			
	2	5	row min.		1	5	node 2		2	1	node 5
1	24	84	24	1	0	84	0	1	24	0	0
2	0	15	0	2	6	15	6	2	0	6	0
3	18	27	18	3	36	27	27	3	18	36	18
4	30	15	15	4	48	15	15	4	30	48	30
5	15	0	0	5	21	0	0	5	15	21	15
6	68	24	24	6	92	24	24	6	68	92	68
7	22	20	20	7	34	20	20	7	22	34	22
8	17	10	10	8	23	10	10	8	17	23	17
9	50	36	36	9	62	36	36	9	50	62	50
10	5	16	5	10	11	16	11	10	5	11	5
Sum			152	Sum			149	Sum			225

$$z = \sum_{i=1}^{10} \sum_{j=1}^{2} a_{ij} w_i d_{ij} = 152 \text{ for nodes 2 and 5}$$

$z = 149$ for nodes 1 and 5

$z = 225$ for nodes 2 and 1

Therefore node 1 is substituted for node 2.

Step 3. Repeat Step 2 for all demand points. Demand point 2 is now no longer in the supply set but from the previous step we know that the combination of nodes 2 and 5 give z = 152 and nodes 2 and 1 give z = 225; since both are greater than the current z of 149, we can move to demand point 3.

Substitute node 3

Current nodes			Sub.	Minimum	
	1	5	3	3,1	3,5
1	0	84	48	0	48
2	6	15	6	6	6
3	36	27	0	0	0
4	48	15	12	12	12
5	21	0	9	9	0
6	92	24	44	44	24
7	34	20	18	18	18
8	23	10	15	15	10
9	62	36	46	46	36
10	11	16	11	11	11
Sum				161	165

Current z = 149

Since both substitutions of node 3 led to an increase in z, no permanent substitution is made.

Substitute node 4

Current nodes			Sub.	Minimum	
	1	5	4	4,1	4,5
1	0	84	64	0	64
2	6	15	10	6	10
3	36	27	12	12	12
4	48	15	0	0	0
5	21	0	5	5	0
6	92	24	28	28	24
7	34	20	10	10	10
8	23	10	11	11	10
9	62	36	38	38	36
10	11	16	11	11	11
Sum				121	177

Current z = 149

When node 4 is substituted for node 5, the new z = 121. Accept it as permanent to make new center locations of 1 and 4.

Note that this is better than the final solution of the alternating algorithm.

Substitute node 5, but note that the combinations 5, 4, and 5, 1 have already been evaluated. They have z values of 177 and 149, respectively. Since both are greater than the current z of 121, neither is permanently substituted.

Substitute node 6

Current node	Sub.		Minimum	
	1	4	6	6,1	6,4
1	0	64	92	0	64
2	6	10	17	6	10
3	36	12	33	33	12
4	48	0	21	21	0
5	21	5	6	6	5
6	92	28	0	0	0
7	34	10	20	20	10
8	23	11	4	4	4
9	62	38	24	24	24
10	11	11	16	11	11
Sum				125	140

Current z = 121.

Neither substitution of node 6 leads to improvement.

The results of the remaining substitutions in the first cycle are summarized in the following table.

z Values for First Cycle of Vertex Substitution Algorithm*

	Nodes substituted for row nodes									
	1	2	3	4	5	6	7	8	9	10
2	☐149☐									
5	225	225	161	☐121☐						
1		152	175	177	177	140	159	144	148	153
4					149	125	138	140	203	215

*Initial z (for nodes 2 and 5) = 152.

Start a second cycle. Supply centers are nodes 4 and 1 with z = 121.

	2	3	4	5	6	7	8	9
1	133	157	177	140	159	144	148	153
4	225	161	149	125	138	140	203	215

Since no improvement in the value of the objective function was found in the complete cycle, the algorithm terminates. The result is a selection of demand points 1 and 4 to be the supply centers with a total weighted distance of 121.

D. Program ALLOC

Program ALLOC can be used to solve this problem using either of the two algorithms just examined. The input of the raw data matrices is, of course, the same as the description given in

Chapter 2, Section 2E. For the problems discussed here, the control card was simple and involved no particular selections by the user. The problems discussed in this section require that the user describe the analysis he wishes by proper selection of the control options available. The control card (numbered 6 in Chapter 2, 2E) follows the weighted data deck. It has the following options:

CONTROL CARDS FOR PROGRAM ALLOC

The sets of control cards which follow may be repeated for successive runs. Maximum number of sets is 100.

6-1	1-5	MP	INT	Number of supply centers to be located
	6-10	MALG	INT	Choose algorithm desired; 1=alternating (Maranzana) algorithm; 2=vertex substitution (Teitz and Bart) algorithm
	11-15	IOP	INT	IOP=1 when a constrained solution is desired
	16-20	IOP2	INT	IOP2=1 means that the algorithm will evaluate the source locations and then will terminate
	21-25	MALG2	INT	MALG2=1 means use both algorithms to find solution starting with that specified in columns 6-10.

6-2 Constraint set data. (Ignored if IOP in columns 11-15 of 6-1 is not 1)

  (1) = Constrained location--that is, if started in source locations, or reached during iterations, this location will be forced into the final solution.

  (2) = feasible location--may be chosen in final solution.

  (3) = infeasible location--may not be present in final solution but its demand will influence the solution

  Fields of 1   80I1   IK   INT   Type of constraint. Number of the column refers to the position of that ID in the distance matrix, e.g., "3" in column 75 means the 75th place ID in the distance matrix is an infeasible location.

6-3 Initial supply center ID's

  Fields of 5   16I5   JS   INT   Place ID's of starting "solution."

Here are some examples of control of this program.

<u>Card Columns</u>

	1 2 3 4 5 6 7 8 9	1 0	1 1	1 2	1 3	1 4	1 5	1 6	1 7	1 8	1 9	2 0	2 1	2 2	2 3	2 4	2 5	2 6	2 7	2 8	2 9	3 0
(2)	(1) 2 2 2 5			1 5 2 2				0 0				0 0				0 0					

Problem (1) would be the control cards for the first handworked example in this section. The first card is instructing the program to locate two centers using the

Multi-Facility Location on a Network

alternating algorithm and the second card orders the use of demand points 2 and 5 as starting supply centers. Problem (2) is a control card for the second handworked example with specification in column 10 of the first control card that the vertex substitution algorithm is to be used.

In the example below, control cards are organized, exactly as they would be in the actual use of the program, to make three consecutive analyses on the same data input.

Card Columns

```
                    1 1 1 1 1 1 1 1 1 1 2 2 2 2 2 2 2 2 2 2 3
  1 2 3 4 5 6 7 8 9 0 1 2 3 4 5 6 7 8 9 0 1 2 3 4 5 6 7 8 9 0
-------------------------------------------------------------
(1)         5       1         0         1         0
(2)         2       1 8       4         9         1 3
(3)         6       1         0         0         1
(4)     1 4         1 8       1 1       6         9
(5)         4         2       1         0         0         4
(6) 2 2 2 1 3 2 2 2 2 2 3 3 2 2 2 2 2 2 2 2 2 2 3 3 2 2
(7)         1 5       3       4         1
```

For convenience in describing and interpreting these control cards, they have been numbered (1) through (7). Card (1) instructs the program to simply evaluate the five supply center locations that follow and then to terminate. The 1 in column 20 is providing this instruction. The ID's of the particular centers to be evaluated are found on card (2). Card (3), following immediately after card (2), is therefore instructing the program to perform the analysis described on that card on the same data set analyzed in the previous problem. Card (3) instructs six centers to be located and two algorithms to be used consecutively (1 in col. 25), starting with the alternating algorithm and then the vertex substitution algorithm using the centers from the final iteration of the alternating algorithm as its own starting supply centers. Card (4) gives the ID's of the six supply centers with which the program should commence analysis. The strategy for solution being used in card (3) is a common one: Analysis is starting with the fastest algorithm (the alternating) and then calling the slower algorithm (the vertex substitution) to improve the best solution found by the alternating. Because the substitution algorithm is starting with a good solution, it should require only a few iterations to converge on its own solution. Since it never makes a permanent substitution unless the value of the objective function has declined, the result of this strategy will never be worse, and frequently will be better than using either algorithm alone.

Card (5) is calling for an analysis of the same data set as the two previous problems, but the 1 in col. 15 is indicating that a "constrained" solution is desired. Constraints on the solution are imposed by the user. For every demand point there must then be a constraint indicating that a particular point must be in the final solution set; may be in the solution set if selected by the algorithm, (a feasible site); or must never be in the solution set, (an infeasible site). When a point must be in the solution set, then its ID should be among the starting supply center set. Although infeasible locations will never be

Multi-Facility Location on a Network   133

selected by the algorithm, their weights will be included in the computations that lead to selections between alternate feasible centers. Notice in this case that the vertex substitution algorithm was selected. Either algorithm could have been selected but especially when the number of constraints becomes large, the performance of the alternating algorithm declines rapidly. This is an example of how the alternating algorithm is less robust than the vertex substitution one. Card (6) specifies the constraints, one for each demand point. It is assumed here that the data set being used has 28 demand points. The constraints use the column numbers to reference the data set ID's. Thus whatever constraint is found in the fourth column refers to the ID of the fourth place in the inter-point distance matrix. Card (6) is thus stating that the fourth place in the distance matrix must occur in the final solution and that the 5th, 12th, 13th, 25th and 26th places must not be in the final solution. Since four places in all are to be located (card (5)), the algorithm must select the remaining 3 supply centers from the remaining demand points.

E. Transformations of the Distance Matrix

A further range of problems may be studied by transformation of the input distance matrix. If the desire is to minimize, not average, distance but average (or total) travel time consumed in getting to the supply points, this problem can be solved by substituting travel times for distances in the input matrix.

Similarly, if least cost solutions are desired, then the cost of taking a unit weight between every pair of centers would be the appropriate "distance" matrix. If, furthermore, there were scale economies in shipping in bulk, then the weighted cost matrix incorporating such economies could be prepared prior to analysis by program ALLOC, then dummy weights of one would be used in the subsequent analysis.

Through these examples we have seen how the user of program ALLOC can control the particular analysis desired by careful choice of options on the control cards, and by making transformations of the distance matrix. The homework examples provide opportunities to test these options.

F. Homework Problems

1. a) Take the ten point network for the handworked example and compute the 1, 2 and 3 supply center solution to this problem using the alternating and vertex substitution algorithms each starting with the same supply center locations.

    b) Find the two center problem, constrain demand point #5 to be in the solution and require that demand point numbers 2 and 7 not be in the solution.

2. Suppose that, in the network of the handworked example, the cost of transporting a unit weight of the product required at the demand points from the supply centers is given by the

expression Cost = 1.0 + 2.0 $\sqrt{x}$ where x is the distance the unit weight has to be moved. Use program ALLOC to find the two center supply points that minimize total transport cost to the demand points.

3. Find the 2, 3, and 4 supply center solution to the unweighted demand points for which the distance matrix is given below:

	1	2	3	4	5	6	7	8	9	10	11	12
1	0	17	57	29	43	66	91	67	81	116	86	81
2	17	0	74	42	26	49	92	68	64	117	87	88
3	57	74	0	46	62	102	38	56	91	69	66	76
4	29	42	46	0	16	56	62	38	54	87	57	58
5	43	26	52	16	0	40	66	42	38	91	61	62
6	66	69	102	67	40	0	97	73	38	116	86	72
7	91	92	38	72	66	97	0	24	59	37	28	42
8	67	68	56	38	42	73	24	0	35	49	19	20
9	81	64	91	54	38	38	59	35	0	78	48	34
10	116	117	69	87	91	116	37	49	78	0	30	44
11	86	87	65	57	61	86	28	19	48	30	0	14
12	87	88	76	58	62	72	42	20	34	44	14	0

Source: A. J. Scott, 1971, p. 133.

(2) <u>Minimizing the Maximum Distance to Closest Supply Center in a System</u>

A. <u>The Problem</u>

For some kinds of problems greater importance is attached to locating the supply centers so that the farthest distance of any demand point from its closest supply center is minimum. This is sometimes referred to as "the welfare criterion" since it focuses attention on the level of spatial accessibility of the most disadvantageously located demand center in the system. A more functional designation of this criterion is the "MINIMAX" criterion. It is a common criterion for the location of emergency facilities where critical response times are often identified and stated to be necessary for an "acceptable" level of spatial service to exist. As with the problem of minimizing average distance, transformation of the inter-point distance matrix prior to analysis will lead to the minimization of alternative criteria. For example, if inter-point travel times are input, then the MINIMAX solution will be the location of centers that minimize the maximum travel time to a supply center. If inter-point costs are input in lieu of distances, the MINIMAX solution will locate centers to minimize the maximum cost incurred by any supply center in servicing any of its demand points--or vice-versa. Unlike the last problem, this criterion is not one in which we can know that solutions exist at nodes rather than on arcs between nodes. In fact there is every reason to believe that the true MINIMAX solution would rarely coincide with nodes on the network. Therefore, only by stating the problem as one of specifically finding the nodes that minimize the maximum service distance can one use procedures that evaluate alternative combinations of nodes. For many problems, this interpretation is quite realistic.

B. Solution Methods

   (i) Intuitive

This problem is probably easier to solve intuitively than the problems discussed earlier since weighting of the demand points is not a part of the problem. In addition, the MINIMAX criterion has a well-known geometrical outcome for the pure conditions of a fine network of routes and no boundaries to the study area--in such conditions, the optimal solution is a triangular point lattice. Granted that real problems never fulfill these pure conditions, they are frequently close enough for this geometrical analogy to hold so that an imaginary triangular point lattice "fitted" to the node network is a good approximation of the solution required. Indeed, rotation of the imaginary lattice will frequently give a large range of possible solutions that have values of the objective function that are close to one another. Try solving the five center location problem for the 33 metropolitan cities used in Chapter 3.

   (ii) Numerical

We have previously claimed that the alternating class of algorithms are versatile in that the alternating concept can be made to work many ways. Can you see how it can be organized to solve the MINIMAX problem? Before studying the steps of the algorithm below, try to formulate the steps on the basis of your knowledge of the alternating concept.

Step 1. Select an arbitrary set of demand points as the supply centers.

Step 2. Partition the remaining demand points into groups around their closest supply point; compute the MINIMAX distance.

Step 3. Find by inspection of each group, that node within the group whose maximum distance to the furthest demand point within the group is least; designate that node as the new supply point.

Step 4. Return to step 2 and re-partition the points around the new supply centers, compute the MINIMAX distance. If the groups are the same as in the previous partitioning, terminate; otherwise, go on to step 3.

C. Handworked Example

For convenience, we take the data for the network in Section 1, C(i), Fig. 4.5, and in step 1, let us select the initial supply centers 2 and 5 chosen there. In the following table we underline the minimum distances for serving each demand point. The MINIMAX value is then the maximum of these minima. For the starting centers the minimum distance reaches its maximum of 18 for serving demand point 9, (step 2). In step 3 (see table) nodes 2 and 8 were found to be most central to their group (step 2). In step 4 (2nd iteration), partitions of the demand centers are made around nodes 2 and 8. For these new partitions the centers are nodes 2 and 8, and since these were the nodes from which the partitions had been derived, convergence has occurred.

First Iteration

	2	5
1	6	21
2	0	15
3	6	9
4	10	5
5	15	0
6	17	6
7	11	10
8	17	10
9	25	18
10	5	16
Minimax	6	18

Minimax = 18

	1	2	3	10
1	0	6	12	11
2	6	0	6	5
3	12	6	0	11
10	11	5	11	0
Max	12	6	12	11

Minimax = 6 for node 2

	4	5	6	7	8	9
4	0	5	7	5	11	19
5	5	0	6	10	10	18
6	7	6	0	10	4	12
7	5	10	10	0	6	14
8	11	10	4	6	0	8
9	19	18	12	14	8	0
Max	19	18	12	14	11	19

Minimax = 11 for node 8

Second Iteration

	2	8
1	6	23
2	0	17
3	6	15
4	10	11
5	15	10
6	17	4
7	11	6
8	17	0
9	25	8
10	5	12
Minimax	10	10

Minimax = 10

	1	2	3	4	10
1	0	6	12	16	11
2	6	0	6	10	5
3	12	6	0	4	11
4	16	10	4	0	11
10	11	5	11	11	0
Max	16	10	12	16	11

Minimax = 10 for node 2

	5	6	7	8	9
5	0	6	10	10	18
6	6	0	10	4	12
7	10	10	0	6	14
8	10	4	6	0	8
9	18	12	14	8	0
Max	18	12	14	10	18

Minimax = 10 for node 8

Optimal Location of Facilities

The solution for the network is to make demand points 2 and 8 the supply centers with the maximum distance of any point in this system from a center being 10.

D. Program ALLOC

Program ALLOC can be manipulated to find the MINIMAX solution using the alternating algorithm. The control cards are set up as in the last example (Page 124) with the exception that in Column 10 of the first control card, a 3 indicates that the MINIMAX analysis is to be performed. Control cards are shown below for the data of the handworked example to perform two consecutive MINIMAX analyses using nodes 2 and 5 as starting locations in the first case and nodes 3 and 6 to start the analysis in the second case.

Example of control cards setup (to follow data for Program ALLOC) to solve the MINIMAX location problem.

Card Columns

1	2	3	4	5	6	7	8	9	10	11	12	13	14	15	16	17	18	19	20	21	22	23	24	25	26	27	28	29	30
				2					3					0					0					0					
		2							5																				
				2					3					0					0					0					
		3							6																				

E. Homework Problems

1. Use the alternating algorithm to solve for the data in the handworked example, the MINIMAX distance for three supply centers.

(3) <u>Minimizing the Number of Centers required for every Demand Point to be within a Critical Distance of a Supply Point</u>

A. The Problem

Sometimes the location problem begins with an agreement about the maximum distance that the furthest demand point should be from a supply center. The problem, then, is to find the required number of supply centers and their locations so that every demand point is so served.

B. Solution Method

Toregas and ReVelle (1972) have developed a matrix "reduction" method for solving this problem. It is a solution method that almost invariably gives the best solution, but occasionally leaves the problem without a complete solution. It always simplifies the problem. It is an interesting method because it is both computationally simple and intuitively reasonable.

The reduction process begins with a matrix showing which demand points are within the critical distance of every potential demand point. The process then eliminates from further consideration every demand point which would be within the critical distance of the same potential supply points as other demand points, but which is also within the critical distance of other supply centers that are unable to serve the other demand points. The rationale for eliminating such centers is that demand points such as the latter must be served to satisfy the objective function and that whichever supply center is selected to serve them would also serve the demand points that have been eliminated. Eliminated points need no further consideration since serving the other points ensures that they also will be served. The handworked example will clarify this step--called row reduction. The second step of the process eliminates from further consideration those potential supply centers that would serve a given set of demand points when it can be shown that some other potential supply center could serve the same set of demand points plus an additional number of demand points. Clearly nothing is lost by eliminating these centers from further consideration.

C. <u>Handworked Example</u>

Let us again take the data of the network of Section (i) which has ten demand points. In Section 1C(i), Fig. 4.5, we found the distance that the furthest point would be from a supply center if only two such centers were to be located and if the objective function were to minimize this distance. The solution of the alternating method to that problem was a distance of ten. In this problem, let us assume that it has been decided that a distance of ten units is the farthest acceptable distance of any demand point from its closest supply center that we wish to know how many such centers are required, and where they should be located such that this criterion is met. This is an example of the matrix reduction method. Step 1 consists of forming a binary matrix indicating which demand points (rows) would be within the critical distance of every potential supply center (column). In this step every demand point is a potential supply center.

First Step of Matrix Reduction Method for Finding Minimum Number of Centers within a Critical Distance of all Demand Points.

First Iteration:

	1	2	3	4	5	6	7	8	9	10
1	✓	✓								
2	✓	✓	✓	✓						✓
3			✓	✓	✓	✓		✓		
4			✓	✓	✓	✓	✓	✓		
5				✓	✓	✓	✓	✓	✓	
6					✓	✓	✓	✓	✓	
7	✓	✓	✓	✓	✓	✓				✓
8					✓	✓	✓	✓	✓	
9								✓	✓	
10	✓						✓			✓

Row Reductions: Row 2 is eliminated by row 1. Notice that no matter which supply center serves demand point 1, demand point 2 will be served. Since demand point 1 must be served to satisfy the objective function, demand point 2 can be eliminated from further consideration as a point to be served. Using the same logic, row 4 can be eliminated because of row 3--any center that serves 3 will also serve 4; 5 is eliminated by 6; 7 is eliminated by 6; and row 8 by row 9. We are now ready for the second step of the matrix reduction algorithm which involves the elimination of unnecessary supply centers (column reduction) by operating on the reduced matrix.

Second Step in the Matrix Reduction: Elimination of Surplus Supply Centers

Potential Supply Centers

		1	2	3	4	5	6	7	8	9	10
demand	1	√	√								
points	3		√	√	√	√		√			
(remaining	6			√	√	√	√	√			
after row	9							√	√		
reduction)	10		√					√			√

Column Reductions: Potential supply center 7 dominates center 5 in that it serves every point that 5 serves plus some others. Point 5 is therefore eliminated. By the same rule 7 dominates 4 and 4 is eliminated; 8 eliminates 9; 7 eliminates 10 and 6; and 2 eliminates both 1 and 3.

Second Iteration: Row Reduction

Potential Supply Centers

		2	7	8
demand	1	√		
points	3	√	√	
	6		√	√
	9			√
	10	√	√	

In the reduced matrix, row 9 eliminates row 6, and 1 eliminates both 3 and 10. The matrix that remains is:

Potential Supply Centers

		2	7	8
demand	1	√		
points	9			√

Since center 7 is serving none of the demand points remaining, it can be eliminated and the 2 x 2 matrix that remains can be reduced no further. It tells us that the solution to the problem

Multi-Facility Location on a Network   145

of serving every demand point on our network within 10 distance units of a supply center is to locate two supply centers at demand points 2 and 8. Note that this was the solution we had previously found by the alternating algorithm, when we solved the MINIMAX problem for the two center case.

D. Homework Problems

1. Find the minimum number of centers and their location to place every demand point in the network shown below within three distance units of a supply center.

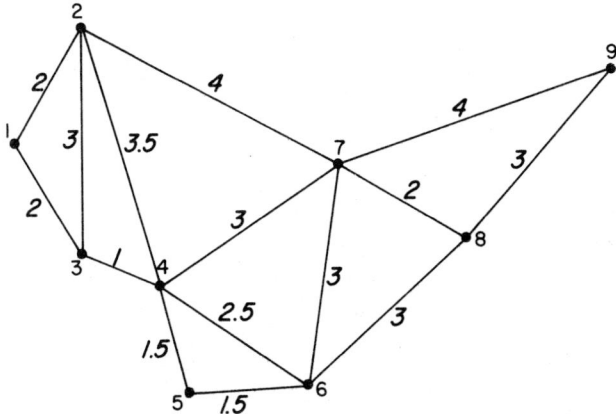

Source: Toregas and ReVelle, 1972.

(4) Minimizing Average Distance Subject to a Maximum Distance Constraint

A. The Problem

Some location problems are formulated in such a way that they combine two of the objectives we have already discussed.

These objectives can be viewed as extreme points of a continuum (see diagram). At one end is the case where locations are

```
    Minimizing average                    MINIMAX
    distance solution                     solution

     1   2   3   4   5   6   7   8   9   10
     ─   ─   ─   ─   ─   ─   ─   ─   ─   ──
```

selected to reduce the total distance travelled in the system. According to this criterion, no attention is given to reducing the maximum distances in the system. When the demand points are weighted, this can result in peripheral points with small weight being long distances from their supply center. At the other end of the continuum is the case where all efforts are made to keep the farthest distance small but no effort is made to keep the total distance travelled in the system small. Frequently policy makers wish to make a compromise between these objectives. Ideally they want to see total distance minimized but as a practical necessity and in justice to those who will be most disadvantageously located with respect to the centers they choose, they will place some constraint on the farthest distance anyone should be from a center. This compromise can be at any point along the continuum. If the constraint distance is set very long, then it may have no effect on the locations selected under the pure distance minimization criterion. On the other hand, the distance constraint may be set so short that the only feasible solution is the minimax solution.

Multi-Facility Location on a Network 147

B. Solution Method

One method of solution is a modification of the vertex substitution method described previously. Recall that this method applied to the total distance minimization criterion began by forming a weighted distance matrix indicating in each cell what the weighted distance would be if the column node were to be the supply center for the corresponding row node. The nodes in both cases are the total set of demand points. Now, whenever the inter-point distance in a cell is greater than the distance constraint, the substitution of the column node should never result in that node serving the corresponding row demand point. A simple transformation of the weighted distance matrix will ensure that the computations described earlier would never allow such a substitution to become permanent. This transformation makes the weighted interpoint distance infinity whenever the column node (a potential supply center) is greater than the maximum distance constraint from the corresponding row node. Then, solving to minimize the total distance separation in the system by the vertex substitution method on this transformed matrix will provide the desired constrained distance solution.

C. Handworked Example

We have previously computed the minimum distance criterion solution for the data on Page 138. The solution had a z value of 121 with nodes 1 and 4. The maximum distance was 19 units from node 4 to node 9. Then in Section (2) we solved the MINIMAX problem for the same data and found a solution which had a maximum distance of 10 units with nodes 2 and 8 as supply centers. The weighted distance for this solution (z) = 131. We can thus conclude that the 8.3 percent decrease in efficiency in the MINIMAX solution was the price paid for minimizing the maximum distance in the system. Suppose we set the objective function to minimize the total distance travelled in the system subject to the constraint that no demand point is more than 15 units from a supply center. The data is for the weighted case of Section 1C(i).

Step 1. Transform the weighted distance matrix by inserting infinity in each cell whenever the column node is more than the constraint distance from the corresponding row node.

Tranformed Weighted Distance Matrix

Potential Supply Centers

		1	2	3	4	5	6	7	8	9	10
	1	0	24	48	*	*	*	*	*	*	44
	2	6	0	6	10	15	*	11	*	*	5
	3	36	18	0	12	27	33	27	45	*	33
	4	*	30	12	0	15	21	15	33	*	33
	5	*	15	9	5	0	6	10	10	*	*
demand	6	*	*	44	28	24	0	40	16	48	*
points	7	*	22	18	10	20	20	0	12	28	12
	8	*	*	15	11	10	4	6	0	8	12
	9	*	*	*	*	*	24	28	16	0	*
	10	11	5	11	11	*	*	6	12	*	0

Legend: * = infinity--distance greater than 15

Multi-Facility Location on a Network

First Iteration:

Step 1. Select initial supply centers that are feasible. Note that in past examples we began with nodes 2 and 5, but in this case these provide an infeasible solution since the weighted distance from both points to demand point 9 is infinity (see table). In the computerized version of this algorithm, it is possible to start with an infeasible solution and a feasible solution will be found (if one exists). In this case, however, we will choose a starting set of centers that are feasible; for example, nodes 1 and 6. Node 6 is the first potential supply center that can combine with node 1 to give a feasible solution. The value of z for this combination is computed in the table below. The substitution process is also demonstrated there.

Vertex Substitution process for distance constraint functions.

	Supply Centers		row
	1	6	min.
1	0	*	0
2	6	*	6
3	36	33	33
4	*	21	21
5	*	6	6
6	*	0	0
7	*	20	20
8	*	4	4
9	*	24	24
10	11	*	11
Sum	z = 125		

	Substitute node 7 for 6		row
	1	7	min.
1	0	*	0
2	6	11	6
3	36	27	27
4	*	15	15
5	*	10	10
6	*	40	40
7	*	0	0
8	*	6	6
9	*	28	28
10	11	6	6
Sum	z = 138		

	Substitute node 7 for 1		row
	7	6	min.
1	*	*	*
2	11	*	11
3	27	33	27
4	15	21	15
5	10	6	6
6	60	0	0
7	0	20	0
8	6	4	4
9	28	24	24
10	6	*	6
Sum	z = *		

Substituting node 7 for node 6 leads to an increase in the objective function to 138, while substituting it for node 1 leads to an infeasible solution. In neither case is it worth substituting permanently. The z values for the computations in the first cycle are summarized below.

	1	2	3	4	5	6	7	8	9	10
1	x	122								
6	x	*	*	*	*		x	146	131	170	*
2			129	*	*	x	*	*	*	149

Note that the first substitution in the first cycle leads to an improvement of the objective function from 125 to 122. This is when node 2 is substituted for node 1. When 2 is substituted for node 6, the solution is infeasible. Therefore, the new supply center set is 6 and 2. When all remaining nodes (3 through 10) are substituted, no improvement in z is found so the second cycle begins with nodes 2 and 6. After node 1 has been substituted without improvement in z, (1,2, is infeasible and 1,5 has z = 125), there is no need to go further since from the previous cycle, we know that all single node substitutions beyond this point lead to no improvements in z. The solution is therefore to select nodes 6 and 2 for a z value of 122 and a maximum distance of 12. The solution therefore satisfies our distance constraint of 15. Note that by sacrificing only one unit weighted distance in our objective function criterion, we have found a solution in which the farthest distance is only twelve units compared with a maximum distance of 19 in the

Multi-Facility Location on a Network 151

solution which had no maximum distance constraints. One can imagine how policy makers might find this latest solution more desirable than the pure distance minimizing solution.

The solution to this problem gives us insights into how these location problems are frequently approached. It is common to ask what the effects would be of adopting a certain objective function. It is one of the advantages of computerized solutions that alternative criteria can be evaluated easily and the results compared. We can plot the rise of the objective function as the maximum distance allowed in the system is more severely constrained (Fig. 4.6).

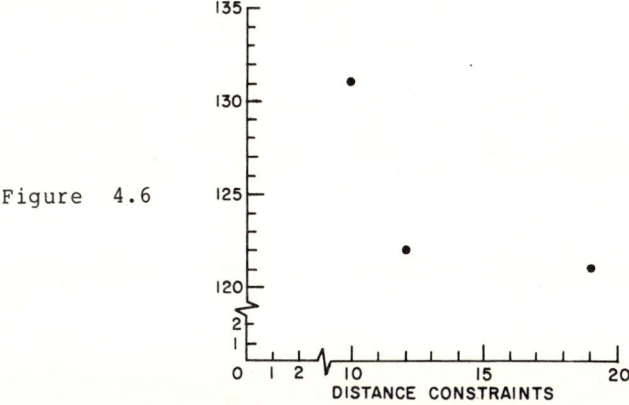

Figure 4.6

D. Program ALLOC

Program ALLOC can be used to compute solutions to problems involving minimizing distance subject to a distance constraint. The raw data section is input as with previous problems. The control cards indicate that this form of problem is to be solved and subsequent cards indicate specifically the value of the distance constraint desired. Several distance constraints (up to 30) can be solved in one run. One rule that must always be followed is that the constraint values must be input in descending order so that large values are solved prior to the smaller values.

CONTROL CARD	Columns
(1) Number of supply centers to be located	1-5
put 2 (for vertex substitution algorithm)	10
Put 1 if constrained solution desired (see sec. 1D)	15
0	20
0	25
Number of distance constraints	26-30
(2) Constraint set data goes here if 1 in col. 15, otherwise ignore.	1-80
(3) Initial supply center ID's - as stated in columns 1-5 of control card 1.	1-5 6-10 11-15 etc.
(4) Distance constraints - as many as stated in columns 26-30 of control card 1. These must go from high to low and be in same units as distance data matrix.	1-5 6-10 11-15 etc.

Example Control Cards for Program ALLOC

Columns of control cards.

```
                    1 1 1 1 1 1 1 1 1 1 2 2 2 2 2 2 2 2 2 2 3
1 2 3 4 5 6 7 8 9 0 1 2 3 4 5 6 7 8 9 0 1 2 3 4 5 6 7 8 9 0
---------------------------------------------------------------
        2           2           0           0           0     1
        1           6
    1 5
        2           2           0           0           0     1
        2           5
    1 5
        2           2           0           0           0     3
        2           5
    2 0       1 5           9
```

These example control cards instruct the program to make three sets of analyses on the same data. The controls here refer to the handworked example. The first set (of three cards) instructs it to locate two centers starting with nodes 1 and 6 with one distance constraint with a value of 15. The second set specifies a similar problem starting though with nodes 2 and 5. The distance constraint is as before. We noted in the handworked section that nodes 2 and 5 represented an infeasible solution when the distance constraint is 15. Nevertheless, the computational code of the program is written so that a feasible solution (if one exists) will first be found and then improved upon during subsequent cycles. The last three cards instruct the program to find the best two supply centers, starting with nodes 2 and 5 and to compute solutions for three distance constraint values of 20, 15 and 9 respectively. We know from the worked example in Section 3C that a feasible solution does not exist for two centers within a distance constraint of 9 units. The program will identify that this is the case and write a note that the solution is infeasible.

E. Homework Problems

1. Take the data matrix in Section 1F(3) (with 12 points) and use program ALLOC to compute the three supply centers that would minimize total travel subject to the constraint that no demand point would be farther than 55 units from its closest supply point.

2. Constrain the problem above so that node 12 is in the solution set and node 2 is not.

Chapter 5 - Shortest Paths Through a Network

A. The Problem

Location problems in which selections must be made from nodes on a route structure require knowledge of the shortest distances between all pairs of points. When location solutions are needed for minimum cost criteria, the costs of taking a unit between all pairs of points are required. In other cases the shortest travel times between pairs of points are required. It is easy to find these in small networks when the information is available between directly connected places but more difficult when the network becomes large.

B. Solution Methods

A variety of methods has been developed for efficiently computing these shortest paths. Described below is the most efficient of the "tree-searching" methods developed by Dijkstra (1959). The approach in such methods is to take a single node

and to compute the shortest paths of all other nodes to it.
Repetition of this process for all nodes gives the full matrix of
interpoint distances. Dijkstra's method is a labelling process
of all nodes that begin an iteration in the state of being
"temporary" with infinitely large distances attached to them.
Through the systematic procedure described below, become labelled
"permanent" when it has been established that the distances
associated with them are the shortest distances to the node being
studied. The re-labelling procedure starts by pivoting on the
beginning node (J) and re-labelling all the nodes directly
connected with it with their associated distances as temporary
"shortest" distances. The node associated with the smallest of
these distances is permanently re-labelled for there can be no
shorter way of connecting these two points. The next step pivots
on this most recently declared permanent node (K) and the
smallest of the distances of the re-labelled temporary nodes
directly connected with K or the sum of the distance from J to K
plus the distance from K to each of the nodes directly connected
with it that are not yet permanent. Whichever node (I) is
associated with this smallest distance is made permanent; its
distance from J is the shortest path from it to J. This Ith node
now becomes the new pivot node K and the last step is repeated.
This process continues until all the nodes are declared
permanent. Their distances are the shortest path distances
desired.

Shortest Paths Through a Network   157

   Ostresh (1973) has summarized the logic:

   Initially all nodes are tentatively set to infinity. After
   the following steps all labels are permanent and represent
   actual shortest paths.

   (1)   Declare NODE(J) permanent

   (2)   K = J

   (3)   NODE(I) = minimum (NODE(I),NODE(K)+D(I,K))
         (D(I,K) is the direct distance between nodes
         I and K, and this is repeated for all nodes
         directly connected with K and not yet
         permanent)

   (4)   Find minimum of tentative nodes (say
         NODE(I))

   (5)   Declare NODE(I) permanent

   (6)   K = I

   (7)   If all NODES are not yet permanent,
         go to step 3.

Shortest Paths by Combinations of Route Nodes. Location problems

often exist in environments where a variety of route nodes are

found. Different classes of roads, for example, from interstate

highways to dirt roads may be independently coded with the

knowledge that for some kinds of location problems only distances

on one class of road are relevant while in other problems the

shortest of any combination of two or more route nodes are

relevant. This tree searching method can be adapted to solve

these problems. The solution involves pre-processing of the

directly connected link data to eliminate data not relevant for a

specified combination of route types and to select the shortest

directly connected distance from among the several admissible route types. After this pre-processing is complete the logic of the algorithm is unaffected by this reinterpretation of the problem.

C. <u>Handworked Example</u>

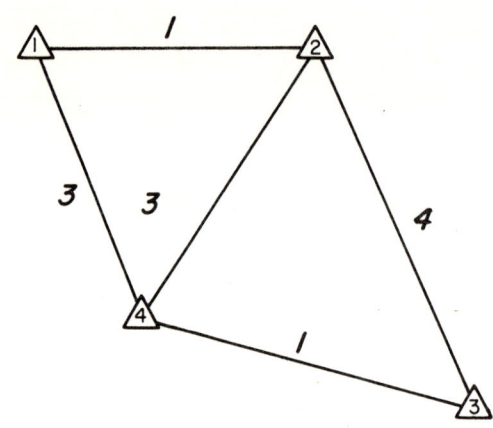

Input Data

	1	2	3	4
1	0	1	4	3
2	1	0		
3	4		0	
4	3			0

Computed shortest paths from node 1.

	1	2	3	4
1	0	1	x	3
2	1	0	4	3
3	x	4	0	1
4	3	3	1	0

<u>Problem</u>: Find the shortest paths from node 1 to all other nodes.

Step 1. Set N1 = 0 and permanent. Denote permanency as <u>0</u>. Enter table. Set remaining nodes at infinity and temporary. Denote temporary as <u>∞</u>.
K = 1.

Step 2. Find places directly connected with N1:N2 and N4.
N2 = min (N2,N1+D(2,1)) = min (∞,0+1) = <u>1</u>
N4 = min (N4,N1+D(4,1)) = min (∞,0+3) = <u>3</u>

Shortest Paths Through a Network   159

Step 3. Make permanent minimum of temporary distances.

   min (N2,N4) = min (1,3) = 1

   N2 = 1 . Enter table.

   K = 2

Step 4. Find places directly connected with N2 that are not yet
         permanent: N4 and N3

   N4 = min (N4,N2+D(4,2)) = min (3,1+3) = 3

   N3 = min (N3,N2+D(3,2)) = min (∞,1+4) = 5

Step 5. Make permanent minimum of temporary distances. Min
         (N4,N3) = 3.

   N4 = 3 . Enter table.

   K = 4

Step 6. Find places directly connected with N4, not yet
         permanent: N3.

   N3 = min (N3,N4 + D(3,4)) = min (5,3+1)= 4

   N3 = 4 . Enter table.

D. Program SPA

Program SPA written by Ostresh (1973) computes shortest paths through a network from input data which describes the distances between directly connected nodes. Provision is also made for distinction to be made in the input data between different route nodes so that combinations of these nodes can be made through use of the control cards. The output is either a matrix of shortest paths between all pairs of points (which can be printed or punched or written on tape) or distances from specified nodes to all other nodes. The punched distance matrix is in a form suitable for input to program ALLOC.

PURPOSE:

    DETERMINE SHORTEST PATHS THROUGH A NETWORK BETWEEN ALL PAIRS OF NODES OR BETWEEN A SPECIFIED SUB-SET OF NODES AND ALL OTHER NODES, VIA SPECIFIED TRAVEL MODES

INPUT REQUIREMENTS:

1. TITLE CARD
2. CONTROL CARD
3. NODE SUB-SET CARD(S)   (OPTIONAL)
4. DATA CARDS
5. END CARD

INPUT CARD FORMATS:

```
C
C    ***                                                      ***
C    ***   NOTE:  RIGHT ADJUST ALL INPUT (EXCEPT TITLE)        ***
C    ***                                                      ***
C
C
C    TITLE CARD                       (1CA8)
C        COLUMNS
C          1-80         ANY TITLE
C
C
C    CONTROL CARD                     (I4,I1,I2,I3,I5,L5,12I5)
C        COLUMN
C          1-4          DATA SET REFERENCE NUMBER FOR READ UNIT, IF
C                       INPUT IS BY TAPE, DISK, CR DRUM; BLANK
C                       OTHERWISE
C           5           PUNCH 1 IN COL. 5 IF INPUT IS BY TAPE, DISK,
C                       OR DRUM AND IS TO BE MODIFIED BY CARD INPUT.
C                       OTHERWISE, LEAVE BLANK
C          6-7          PUNCH 1 IN COL. 7 IF ACTUAL SHORTEST PATHS
C                       ARE TO BE PRINTED; OTHERWISE LEAVE BLANK
C          8-10         PRINT/PUNCH OPTION FOR DISTANCE MATRIX:
C                         PRINT ONLY -- LEAVE BLANK
C                         PRINT AND PUNCH --'1' IN COL. 10
C                         PUNCH ONLY--'2' IN COL. 10
C         11-15         NUMBER OF NODES TO BE READ IN, IF OUTPUT
C                       IS TO LIST SHORTEST PATHS TO AND FROM A
C                       SPECIFIED SUB-SET OF NODES; BLANK OTHERWISE
```

```
C                   16-20     'TRUE' --IF ECHO CHECK OF DATA CARDS DESIRED
C                             'FALSE' -- OTHERWISE
C                   21-25     FIRST TRAVEL MODE
C                   26-30     SECOND TRAVEL MODE, IF ANY; BLANK OTHERWISE
C                   31-35     THIRD TRAVEL MODE, IF ANY; BLANK OTHERWISE
C                             -- ETC., UP TO 12 TRAVEL MODES IN FIELDS OF
C                             FIVE
C
C
C         NODE SUBSET CARD(S)           (8(4X,I6))        (OPTIONAL)
C            COLUMNS
C              1-10    FIRST SPECIFIED NODE IDENTIFICATION NUMBER
C             11-20    SECOND SPECIFIED NODE I. D.
C             21-30    THIRD SPECIFIED NODE I. D., ETC., UP TO 8
C                      SPECIFIED NODES IN FIELDS OF 10.
C                      IF MORE NODES DESIRED, GO TO TWO OR MORE
C                      CARDS, 8 NODES TO A CARD
C
C         NOTE:   NODE IDENTIFICATION NUMBERS ARE TO CONSIST OF ANY
C                 6-DIGIT INTEGER OTHER THAN 000000 UP TO SIX
C
C
C         DATA CARDS                 (2(4X,I6),12(5X))--MODIFIED BY
C                                     TRAVEL MODES DURING EXECUTION
C            COLUMNS
C              1-10    IDENTIFICATION NUMBER OF NODE A
C             11-20    IDENTIFICATION NUMBER OF NODE B
C             21-25    DISTANCE BETWEEN NODE A AND B VIA TRAVEL
C                      MODE 1, IF ANY; BLANK OTHERWISE
C             26-30    DISTANCE BETWEEN NODE A AND NODE B VIA TRAVEL
C                      MODE 2, IF ANY; BLANK OTHERWISE
C             31-35    DISTANCE BETWEEN NODE A AND NODE B VIA TRAVEL

C                      MODE 3, IF ANY; BLANK OTHERWISE--ETC., UP TO
C                      12 DISTANCES IN FIELDS OF FIVE
C
C         NOTE:   NODE IDENTIFICATION NUMBERS ARE TO CONSIST OF ANY
C                 6-DIGIT INTEGER OTHER THAN 000000
C
C         NOTE:   DISTANCES ARE TO CONSIST OF ANY INTEGER IN THE
C                 RANGE 0-9999; DECIMAL POINTS ARE NOT PERMITTED
C
C
C         END CARD
C            COLUMNS
C              1-3     PUNCH 'END' IN COLS. 1-3; LEAVE REST OF CARD
C                      BLANK
C
```

Sample Data Input

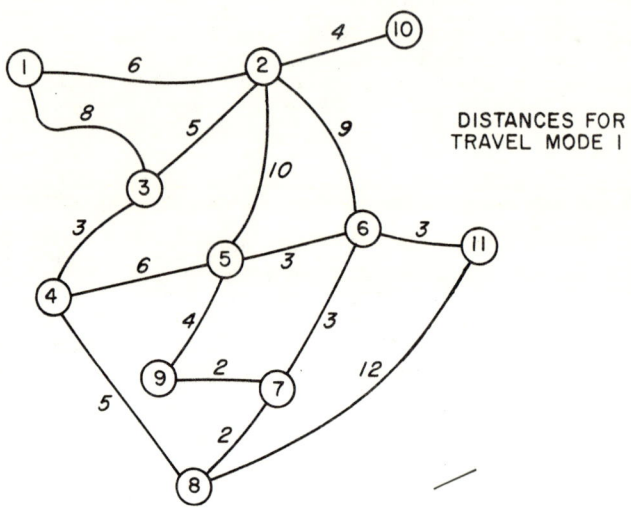

DISTANCES FOR TRAVEL MODE 1

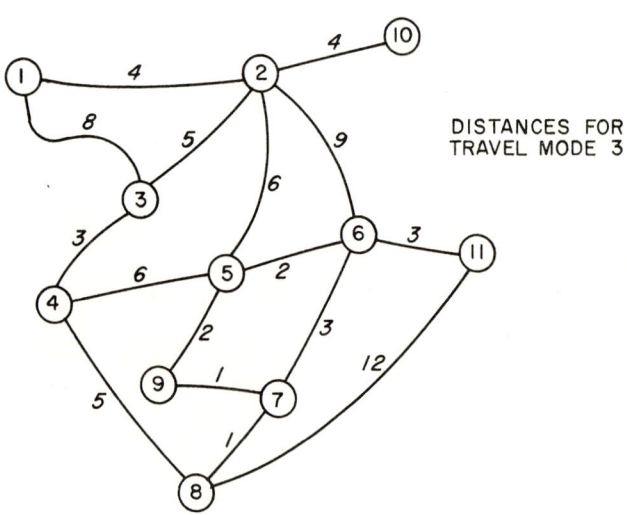

DISTANCES FOR TRAVEL MODE 3

Shortest Paths Through a Network

```
                    1 1 1 1 1 1 1 1 1 1 2 2 2 2 2 2 2 2 2 2 3 3 3 3 3 3
1 2 3 4 5 6 7 8 9 0 1 2 3 4 5 6 7 8 9 0 1 2 3 4 5 6 7 8 9 0 1 2 3 4 5

TITLE CARD -- THIS IS A SAMPLE INPUT FOR 11 POINTS
            1       1             T R U E         1         3
                    1                   2         6                 4
                    1                   3         8                 8
                    2                 1 0         4                 4
                    2                   3         5                 5
                    2                   5       1 0                 6
                    2                   6         9                 9
                    3                   4         3                 3
                    4                   5         6                 6
                    4                   8         5                 5
                    5                   6         3                 2
                    5                   9         4                 2
                    6                 1 1         3                 3
                    6                   7         3                 3
                    7                   9         2                 1
                    7                   8         2                 1
E N D               8                 1 1       1 2               1 2
```

In this example, the first control card after the title card indicates that the paths that the shortest paths take through the network should be printed (col. 7); that the interpoint distance matrix should be both printed and punched; that the input data should be printed (good for checking accuracy of data input); and that the shortest combinations of travel nodes 1 and 3 should be computed. The remaining data cards are the distances for the directly connected links for the two travel nodes in question.

E. Homework Problems

1. Select any geographical study area that interest you and code the network of routes by the various relevant travel modes for input to program SPA. Compute and print the shortest paths and their distances for this area.

REFERENCES

Cooper, L. "Heuristic methods for location-allocation problems." SIAM Review, 1964, 6, 37-53.

Dijkstra, E. W. "A note on two problems in connexion with graphs." Numerische Mathematik, 1959, 1, 269-271.

Drysdale, J. K., and P. J. Sandiford. "Heuristic warehouse location--A case history using a new method." Journal of the Canadian Operational Research Society, 1969, 7, 45-61.

Eilon, Samuel. Distribution Management, Mathematical Modelling and Practical Analysis. New York: Hafner, 1971.

Government of Bihar. "Project report on development of markets in Bihar." Patna, India, 1971.

Harris, C. D. "The market as a factor in the localization of industry in the United States." Annals, Association of American Geographers, 1954, 44, 315-348.

Hindes, C. "The location of intensive coronary care units in Iowa, 1971." Unpublished paper, Department of Geography, University of Iowa, 1971.

Leamer, E. E. "Locational equilibria." Journal of Regional Science, 1968, 8, 229-242.

Maranzana, F. E. "On the location of supply points to minimize transport costs." Operational Research Quarterly, 1964, 15, 261-270.

ReVelle, Charles, David Marksand, and Jon C. Liebman. "An analysis of private and public sector location models." Management Science, 1970, 16, 692-707.

Rushton, G., M. F. Goodchild, and L. M. Ostresh, Jr. (eds.). *Computer Programs for Location-Allocation Problems*. Iowa City, Iowa: University of Iowa, Department of Geography, monograph no. 6, 1973.

Savas, E. S. "Simulation and cost-effectiveness analysis of New York's Emergency Ambulance Service." *Management Science*, 1969, 15, B-608-627.

Scott, A. J. *Combinatorial Programming, Spatial Analysis and Planning*. London: Methuen and Company, 1971.

Teitz, M. B. and P. Bart. "Heuristic methods for estimating the generalized vertex median of a graph." *Operations Research*, 1968, 16, 955-961.

Toregas, C. and C. ReVelle. "Optimal location under time or distance constraints." *Papers, Regional Science Association*, 1972, 28, 133-143.

Whitman, E. S. and W. S. Schmidt. *Plant Relocation: A Case History of a Move*. Management Association, 1966.

206243